WAKE UP & SAVE OUR PLANET!

BLUEPRINT FOR A BETTER WORLD. INTEGRAL APPROACH TO OUR GLOBAL PROBLEMS

MARIANNA FARFALLA

Wake Up & Save our Planet! Blueprint for a better World. Integral approach to solve our global problems. Take Health and Happiness into your Own Hands. Heal yourself and Heal the world.

CONTENTS

Wake Up & Save our Planet!
Blueprint for a better World.
Integral approach to our global problems.

Take Health and Happiness
into your Own Hands.

Heal Yourself
and Heal the World.

I dedicate my message especially to the young children because they are the most wonderful but also the most vulnerable creatures on earth and they deserve a better world!

PREFACE

This book offers a solution for all the global problems we have created — with a disconnected mind — since the industrial revolution.

WHAT YOU FEEL, YOU CAN HEAL!

If you are locked up in your mind,
you remain ignorant and blind
for the real essence of love,
and the Divine Universe above
If you open your heart,
wisdom will be on your part,
joy and happiness will arise
and the world will be a paradise!

Remember the famous remarks of Martin Luther King: "For bad things to happen, it only takes good people to wait for it" or Desmond Tutu: "If you remain impartial in an unjust situation, you have already taken sides and you are supporting injustice".

Together we can break the power of the powerful lobbies and force them to change their policy. What we need – now more than ever – is a revolution of awareness! Together we can bring pressure to bear on the politics to work for peace, health and happiness.

Today, you can take control of your own life and start your own process of self-knowledge and self-realization, and the development of self-love, and love for your fellow human beings and for our planet, 'mother earth'.

So please wake up and do everything you can to save our planet! Stand up and fight against global warming and help to create a circular-sustainable economy.

For me writing this book was a big challenge, a mission that burned inside me. It took me three years to write, because there was always interesting news to work out. At first I wrote two small books, one for the Nuclear Security Summit in The Hague and another for the Climate Change Conference in Paris. Later I decided to put it all together in this book.

I really have to thank my dear friend Wilma Zoetbrood who worked out my handwritten — difficult to read — manuscript. She took care of all the additions on this never-ending story and the layout.

Dear Wilma, thank you for your patience and encouragement!

I also thank a second dear friend, Richard Brown, who controlled the correctness of the English language. I thank my dear friend Ada Frumeau, who studied political science and checked the factual evidence of my book. And last — but not — least, I thank my dear friend (and personal assistant) Monica Reyes for all the research and support she gave to me. - *Marianna Farfalla*

INTRODUCTION

WE ARE FACING THE BIGGEST AND MOST EXCITING CHALLENGE IN THE HISTORY OF MANKIND.

When will we finally realise that we need to make a profound change in order to control this ticking time bomb scenario of a climate crisis that threatens our existence, and the financial crises by which increasingly more people are duped?

If the answer is 'yes', we can turn the tide together, and create a splendid future.

If the answer is 'no, we will end up as the most foolish generation that ever lived on earth. Because even though we were being warned repeatedly, we clearly have been blind to the signs.

In the past 150 years we have unleashed two major revolutions: the industrial and the digital one.

In terms of technology we are incredibly ingenious, and all our inventions have brought about lots of prosperity and a great deal of comfort, but this is all divided very unequal and unfair. In addition our welfare is under threat, and this is because of some of our critical mistakes, like the development of production methods bringing hazardous chemicals in circulation that are harmful for our health, and the use of fossil fuel that is causing global warming. According to me it is absolutely unbelievable that on the level of technological development the human race is extreme bright and intelligent. But on the contrary: on the level of universal knowledge about health & happiness, mankind stays far behind.

Although all this valuable knowledge about loving care for our self, each other and our planet Mother Earth is available, we lost it slowly but surely since the rise of the Industrial Revolution. We were chased out of our houses and were pushed into the factories. We lost the production of our own handcraft and agricultural-provision.

In the beginning men, women and children were exploited to carry out their labor for poverty wages and under barbaric circumstances.

We were no longer masters over our own existence and we lost the precious contact with our intuition, our creativity and with nature. Slowly we became alienated from our True Self and our true needs.

We have to face the reality; we are trapped in a harsh capitalistic system where small parts of the world-population, a few billionaires are having extreme power.

The pressure on the middle-class is getting heavier every day. More and more medium sized enterprises are going bankrupt and the lower-class suffers the most.

In the industrial countries we have developed a system of production and consumption excesses. Thus we have exhausted our natural resources in such a way that the ecological infrastructure has been seriously damaged, to the point where we have endangered our own lives.

Right now there is an urgent need for a third revolution, a revolution of consciousness. So what we need right now is to develop our intuitive intelligence, our wisdom of the heart, to use our technology wisely.

This applies especially to the older generations of men who have been raised and conditioned with a strong sense of rationality, valuing mind over matter, listening to their mind instead of their heart. They operate with a disconnected mind and are not aware of the severe damage they cause.

A DISCONNECTED MIND IS A DANGEROUS MIND!

Men who have not developed their intuition and empathy are not in touch with their True Self and there is a gap between the mind and heart. This is also true for certain 'iron ladies' who have adapted themselves too much to rational male office or boardroom standards.

It's dangerous to operate with a rational, disconnected mind. Let me make this clear: if you develop nuclear energy and **think** it's a right and safe kind of energy, something is **very** wrong because you don't **feel** you're creating huge damage.

This is the result of a materialistic conditioning that has collectively brainwashed people. In our industrialised world, too many people are no longer able to feel. They only **think** they feel.

The Dalai Lama once said that the women should unleash a revolution of consciousness. It is up to them to invite the men to come to their senses.

In the past only women were conditioned to be emotionally sensitive. But they have put up a fight for intellectual development, and gained access to universal suffrage, and higher education. Hence, they now have an advantage over most men. However, this advantage also involves a major risk. As long as the situation stays the same, women are increasingly overburdened since they also have jobs outside their homes, while their husbands are not willing (or cannot) contribute to family-housework and parenthood sufficiently.

Therefore, men should be invited to become aware of the fact they learned to suppress their emotional side and they harm themselves and their family-life if they are not in touch with their intuition and become a workaholic. There are many examples of men that worked so hard that they neglected the needs of their wives/spouses and children. Usually, this type of men comes to awareness when they are forced to step out of the rat race because they become seriously ill. And only then they realize they didn't support their children enough when they needed their father most.

Men have never, en masse, protested against their limited, emotional development, which is odd. As long as men only live a rational life, they are letting themselves down! They always need to be tough and heroic, be responsible for the financial situation of the family, hide their fear and insecurity, and force themselves to perform better every day. That is simply inhuman! No wonder men live an average of five years less than women.

Many men do not realize how precious it is to see their children grow up. Besides this, it is a heavy and responsible job to guide children on their path to maturity in our current complex society. Men often don't know what they are missing in this era of absent fathers, while children really need their fathers while growing up. And last, but certainly not least, our children can teach us so much. Especially babies and toddlers are still very sensitive, spontaneous, honest and creative. They are never bored and completely lose themselves in the games they play. They are mindfulness experts and enjoy life to the fullest.

We, as adults, were forced to get rid of these qualities along the way. Most adults are trapped between unfinished business of the past and their worries for the future, and are no longer capable of experiencing the joy of the moment.

Children help us to connect with our inner child, deeply buried under the armor of everything we were taught to survive in our current society. Being connected to our children, we can learn how to empty our heads and to feel the needs of our hearts again. Together with our children, we can dance, sing, draw or jump around and free the power of our imagination.

But this is not the only harmful result; there is also a danger on a worldwide level.

Men who are not in touch with their intuition and compassion, because there is a gap between their mind and their heart, commit crimes (ranging from deception, fraud and theft to murder) abuse and rape women and children, abuse animals, torture their fellow human beings, lower themselves to committing incest and create pointless wars. On top of it all, they produce dangerous chemicals and nuclear pollution, and allow the use of irresponsible amounts of antibiotics in agriculture, the irresponsible destruction of rainforests, overfishing in our oceans etc. etc. Obviously, also women

commit these crimes, however this group of women is relatively small.

It might occur to you that I'm a man hater. However the opposite is true. Four of the sweetest people I know are men. My relationships with men are better than with women because I have a lot of male character qualities. I would like to point out that, obviously, this doesn't mean all women are both mentally and emotionally developed and all men only mentally. A group of women taking up senior positions is highly mentally developed and work in an industry that once was created by men.

It is important for these women to be aware of their ability to contribute to the wellbeing of humanity if they are capable of connecting their minds with their hearts.

After all, the last thing we need is for women to toughen up. What we do need is for men to soften up.

Fortunately, I also notice a growing new group of men. Men with a more developed emotional side who want to spend as much time with their family as they possibly can and men who are aware of the current dangers we are facing, which made them decide to become sustainable entrepreneurs. In my eyes, this is a very positive development.

I am absolutely convinced of the fact that we can only create a better world if man as much as possible open their hearts and become more sensible and have more respect and appreciation for women.

Now, more than ever, we need men and women who come up with innovation projects that serve the true needs of humanity and give the earth the chance to recover from the huge damage done by people. We need a new 'Silicon Valley'; a so-

called eco-valley, a hotbed for creativity and innovation. If we destroy our nature, we finally destroy ourselves.

In the last century we have destroyed over one third of nature, and dumped an astonishing amount of chemical and nuclear waste. In 2017, these practices have become worse than ever.

WE HAVE TO PROTECT OUR PRECIOUS RAIN FORESTS

We have to make sure the destruction of the rainforest will stop for they are an essential part of our ecological infrastructure and they contain valuable medicinal plants. What's more, they convert carbon dioxide into oxygen which reduces the CO_2 emission.

When consumers decide to buy only paper and wood with a fsc-label they help to save the rainforest.

Moreover, because of our ignorant and wasteful methods of production and consumption we have contributed significantly to the greenhouse effect, to such an extent that the ice sheets and glaciers are melting at an alarmingly fast pace, and that the sea-level is rising.

According to the latest alarming research – carried out by NASA, among others – the permafrost on the Northern Hemisphere appears to be melting much faster than anticipated. The amount of past methane and carbon dioxide emissions is so great, that we are probably too late to limit the greenhouse effect to 2 degrees Celsius.

Because the Arctic ice is melting a large quantity of fresh water is flowing into the Arctic Sea causing the Gulf Stream, which influences weather temperatures in Europe, to slow down its course. This is a disturbingly dangerous development.

"When the Gulf Stream flows slower, it is very likely to result in a new ice age on the Northern Hemisphere, threatening the lives of tens of millions of people." *(From: Demain la Terre, Yannick Monget)*

This fact is confirmed in a secret report by the Pentagon.

What's more, the ice on Greenland is melting rapidly, and this will have a direct effect on the rising of the sea level.

We are already witnessing the appalling effects of climate change in the shape of extreme cold, drought, heavy rainfall and violent storms, hurricanes, whirlwinds, and even typhoons.

How many natural disasters do we need before mankind wakes up and starts to live responsibly?

When will we finally realize that we should respect and protect our planet's ecological infrastructure, because it is the foundation of our existence!

I've been fighting climate change for seventeen years now. Climate change that was mostly caused by our very selves. And the fact that so little people are willing to make an effort to reverse the damage done fills me with despair.

How on earth can you combine the love for your children and grandchildren with such an amount of indifference? It just makes no sense to me! What kind of world do we pass on to our children? No wonder an increasing amount of youngsters end up being alcoholics and drug addicts. Some of them even go into a coma after a night of binge drinking or drug abuse.

Despite stern warnings of climate scientists, powerful lobbies of certain banks and multinationals refuse to change their policy.

There is a consensus among 97% of all the climate scientists that we caused the main part of global warming. In spite of that there is a huge campaign of 'the Republican old boys lobby's network' who spread out dangerous lies in America that climate change does not exist. In my opinion these old boys should have to appear in court, because their misleading campaign creates more climate victims. If you want more information about this issue, I highly recommend you to look at the impressive documentary: 'Before the flood' of Leonardo di Caprio. Many people who saw it, said that it was for them a life-changing experience. Most politicians are not capable of resolving the climate change problem since they are lacking the knowledge and courage to take effective measures.

And most of citizens of the industrialized world still seem to be thinking their happiness is depending on the amount of stuff they buy, because smart and tricky advertising tells them it is.

Being a social scientist, I often wonder what made most people become so passive and apathetic. Whatever happened to the passion and drive to act from the sixties and seventies, the demonstrations I took part in so intensively and frequently myself.

And why was I forced to witness a substantial part of our democratic rights, which we fought so hard for at the time, has been taken away from us?

Is it presumptuous indifference or intellectual lethargy, or are we no longer able to act due to the never ending, wrecking rat race we're all part of?

In my eyes, the main cause is a tremendous lack of consciousness. And the fact that people, who do realize what is going on, are being overwhelmed by fear and the feeling of

being completely powerless, making them feel compelled to bury their heads in the sand instead.

Sometimes, I can hear people complain: "If I would really realize how serious the actual climate catastrophe is, I wouldn't be able to sleep at night."

And there is only one way for me to respond: If we don't take action together now, our country will be history.

WAKE UP! OPEN YOUR EYES AND DO WHAT YOU CAN DO TO SAVE OUR PLANET!

We have to fully realize what is happening to us:

We're all trapped in the same, incredibly large and complex global system, where, to a large extent, we handed over the control of our own lives. We always trusted the government to look after us but they failed to monitor and protect our basic provisions and they are abandoning us to our fate more every day and deliver us at the mercy of free market institutions. So for what reason we have to pay our taxes? Many people feel powerless and used as a pawn in the game of the powerful lobbies of banks and multi-nationals. A painful fact is that the most vulnerable people among us, the ill and handicapped are the biggest victims.

The social structure in the industrial world has lost a lot of the pre-industrial social cohesion and the bureaucratic laws and regulations are too oppressing and paralyzing. School encourages us to use our heads, not our precious intuition and creativity. As a result, we are disconnected from our True Self and our pure intuition and we live in a state of inner disharmony. We let our minds rule our lives and create all kinds of unnecessary problems. We can't stop thinking and worrying and we still don't understand that our biggest and global problems can only be solved by activating our pure intuition and creativity, both so thoroughly inactivated during our upbringing and education.

What we need right now – more than ever – is a revolution of the consciousness. We have to reconnect our heads to our hearts and follow the signals of our pure intuition. We need to use our heads to realise the outcome of these signals. If we do so, deep inside we will feel that together we have to create a sustainable economy that serves our true needs.

So what we need right now is to develop our intuitive intelligence, the wisdom of our hearts, to wisely use our technology.

First of all we have to understand that the underlying cause of all our global problems, including the dramatic climate crisis and the credit crunch, is a crisis of values. In the industrial countries, we educated our children with the wrong materialistic concepts. We should teach them the right universal values.

We have to wake up and understand the importance of living consciously and the meaning of true spirituality.

Living consciously means that you regularly pause and reflect on your way of living and consider the consequences of your lifestyle for yourself, your fellow men and our planet, Mother Earth.

Living a spiritual life involves living consciously and treating yourself, your fellow men and our planet, mother earth, lovingly.

All people on earth have an equal need for food, clothing, housing, education, loving relations and medical care.

Mother Earth offers us all the food we need to stay healthy and happy. But instead of using this gift gratefully, we manipulate our food to an extent where only very little is left of the original nutritive substance and people become needlessly ill.

OUR UNHEALTHY LIFESTYLE CREATES DISEASES OF AFFLUENCE

The way people treat themselves is striking. They treat their car as if it were a sacred cow and themselves as the neglected calf.

Everything has to be sacrificed for this number one status symbol and we spend lots of money to buy and maintain our inanimate 'pet'. How differently do we treat our own bodies; our bodies are rushed, abused and stuffed with unwholesome food and stimulating products like tobacco, alcohol and other drugs.

Our so-called health is not what it appears to be! Many people think they are healthy since they can't actually see the damage done. However, this so-called state of health is not real.

The damage done to your body as a result of an unnatural, stressful lifestyle can be considered a dangerous cumulative effect. Ever more toxins are added until the pres- sure becomes too high and your body breaks down. If you're lucky, you're able to fix the damage. If not, you won't survive. When you start noticing the consequences of this damage and you suffer from chronic fatigue or worse, from diabetes, or a heart attack, your whole world will fall into pieces and you are forced to become aware of your lifestyle and eating habits.

We have developed an unhealthy lifestyle with too much tension and stress, and an unhealthy diet consisting of too

much sugar, refined white flour products, saturated fats, and too much meat.

This lifestyle causes a whole range of so-called diseases of affluence like cancer, diabetes, cardiovascular disease, and obesity. The costs for health care increase worldwide, and become too expensive. Research has shown that we have to eat less meat and lots of fresh vegetables and fruits (preferably biological) to stay healthy. Recent studies of the World Health Organization show that eating regularly processed meat increases the danger of cancer.

There is one effective way to limit these costs: knowledge of healthy food and respect for nature must become part of the school curriculum.

One of the biggest mistakes is throwing away the precious 'coat' of the grain, the husk. It contains urgently needed valuable fibers and minerals. Another mistake is using too much sugar instead of natural sweeteners. Their high carbohydrate levels weaken our immune system, make us fat, disturb our intestinal flora and attribute to developing hypoglycemia and diabetes.

To sweeten our food we can use honey, maple syrup, concentrated fruit syrups or stevia. It's very important to avoid saturated fats and take vital fats especially fish oil and vegetable oil such as primrose oil.

THERE IS ENOUGH FOOD FOR ALL OF US!

If we really understand the fact that we are all brothers and sisters with the same needs and there is enough food for all of us, if we learn to share food and goods in a fair way, only then a new mutual trust will rise and there will be no reason for war.

We developed all the technical knowledge to create paradise on earth but still millions of people are forced to live a daily hell of hunger, war and violence.

So, from a technological point of view, we are incredibly intelligent.

However, from the point of view of universal intelligence, transcending all other forms of knowledge and creating the optimal conditions for a healthy and happy life, we have a long way to go.

Do you ever give thought to the idea of a huge magic engine activating the energy that ensures all animals to use their instincts and people to use their intuition in order to establish balance and harmony on our planet?

Instead of understanding and respecting this magical cycle and allowing Mother Nature to do her important work, we are disturbing this process over and over again.

All our rational intelligence together could never equal the universal intelligence that drives that magical circle of life on earth.

ALL LIFE ON EARTH IS OPERATED BY A UNIVERSAL INTELLIGENCE

This all embracing intelligence ensures that animals follow their instincts and people their intuition. Birds instinctively respond to a signal that they must fly South before the winter is coming. Without that signal they would freeze to death. Just like animals we experience these instinctive signals as well, but we call it intuition. Without intuitive signals people will die an early death as well.

Only in humans this process takes longer than in animals. Human beings become ill first, because they do a lot of things that damage their health, such as overeating or eating an unhealthy diet, smoking, using drugs, drinking too much alcohol and working too hard.

For centuries all problems on earth have been caused by a distinct lack of true spiritual awareness.

Spiritual awareness requires getting to know yourself on a deeper level and reconnecting yourself with the inner source of happiness that you were born with. Pure intuition flows from your True Self, and that intuition will always steer you in the right direction in your life, and will tell you what you should do to stay happy and healthy. Intuition is the voice of your soul and the nature of the soul is endless joy. The soul is also the source of passion and creativity.

When you look at young children you can see that they are still in touch with their inner source of happiness. A baby smiles at you for no particular reason; he just expresses his natural joy.

Children are still unprejudiced. They live in the here and now, they can lose themselves completely in their games, they are creative, and enjoy life to the fullest.

So why are many adults sitting around being bored? Why do they become addicted to their computers, to video games, or their smartphones? Why are they sitting listlessly in front of the TV? How is it possible that happy toddlers turn into zapping zombies?

The reason is that we instil the values of industrial society in our children, and that is wrong. We should help our children to develop their intuition and creativity, and teach them universal values like self-knowledge, self-confidence, sincere

communication, mindfulness (positive thinking), and compassion. Moreover, we should teach them to be conscious, and pass on our knowledge of good food, and how to take good care of our planet.

Instead of paying attention to these important aspects of a healthy and happy life, we block the natural source of happiness and the free flow of pure intuition and creativity in our children, and make them part of a 'collectively brainwashed society' that adheres to the wrong concepts of a materialistic way of life, such as egoism, greed, exploiting others for personal gain, competition, and the importance of outward appearances.

You are expected to keep working as hard as possible. Idleness is not appreciated. On top of that, you are expected to be perfect and cannot afford to make mistakes.

You have to reach the top and participate in the 'rat race', continuously competing with other people.

These things make us insecure. We have become susceptible to manipulation, and are told over and over again that the only way to be happy is to consume as much stuff as possible and to surround ourselves with all kinds of status symbols.

These learned behavior patterns make up the conditional self. Their power makes them able to dominate your life and even make you ill. This prototype of a human being separated itself from the big picture of universal wellbeing and is forced to participate in a large-scale system of maximum production and consumption that causes major global problems such as the climate crisis and the credit crunch. Finally, people forget who they really are and what they really need.

On a superficial level, the way people live their lives fulfil their material needs but they experience an inward emptiness and it is just that soulless feeling that urges us to escape in all kinds of harmful addiction because they lack inspiration, a sense of meaning and a feeling of unity.

It always makes me sad to see that beautiful young children are robbed of their innocence. This does not only happen in the industrialized countries.

Also in lesser developed countries young open-minded and free-spirited children are indoctrinated with wrong values through which they learn about contempt and how to hate other groups. For generations certain so-called religions have propagated violence, and started wars and hate campaigns. Just imagine, for instance, how many people have been killed in God's name? What a terrible aberration!

Don't these people understand that they are making 'their' God appear really bad by doing this? This is the perfect example of how the disconnected mind works that forms a threat to world peace.

Let me get this straight: any religion that sows the seeds of discord and hate has no right to exist.

And any hatemonger is incredibly shortsighted and ignorant, because if you truly believe in God you know that the essence of God is immense and unconditional love.

HOW CAN WE STOP THE CHAIN OF VIOLENCE?

Now you are probably wondering how it is possible that your True Self is the source of so many good qualities and still so much evil takes place in the world.

I am convinced that evil will be only manifested when the good which is naturally present in the newborn child, is disrupted during the family education and school teaching.

When you suppress the intuition and creativity and give negative feedback you undermine the self-confidence of the child and you create a basis for destructive behavior.

First of all we must understand that the majority of mankind does not want war, they want to live in peace and harmony. Yet millions of people in history became victims and today the bloodshed goes on and on. **How is that possible?**

We must not forget that wars are often triggered by megalomaniac dictators with a psychopathic personality like Adolf Hitler, Pol Pot, Idi Amin and so on.

At the moment there are even terroristic groups who commit horrific attacks by blowing themselves up with bomb-girdles as Isis, Al Quaida, Al Shabaab, etc.

They think there are 72 virgins waiting in heaven as a reward.

When you believe such a ridiculous delusion you have a twisted, dangerous mind and you bring unbelievable pain and damage to yourself and your victims.

There are other Holy Beliefs that make much more sense: suppose that you believe in Reincarnation and the laws of Birth & Rebirth, like they do in Eastern traditions like Hinduism and Buddhism, then your conception of life will be totally different. Then you believe there is not only one life, but after your death, you will be born again.

Life is a school and each life gives you new chances to learn 'by trial and error' and to become slowly and surely a better person.

This also means that all your good and bad behavior of your actual life will have good or bad consequences in your next life.

According to this approach all these repulsive terrorist don't arrive in heaven surrounded by 72 virgins, but they have to face 'The hell they created and 'fight against 72 demons'. They have 'to drain the bitter cup', until they really realize the impact of the tremendous pain and sorrow they caused.

So for all the 'religious maniacs' I have a special message: raise your consciousness. Be aware of the incredible damage you caused; ask the holy God (or the holy Allah) forgiveness; and finally stop this blood shedding!

The negative effect of violent films

On top of that the film industry & television-production expose their public to films with repulsive violence. Moreover children are exposed to violent computergames. I am convinced that committing violent acts is also encouraged by films and crime thrillers with an abundance of violence. To me, all this violence is repulsive and dis- gusting, when I see it I have to cloth my eyes and ears, otherwise I will be touched by nausea. I often wonder which type of 'invisible power' organizes all this violence in films? Is it the arms-factory lobby? Are there other lobby's who want to increase our fear, because fearful citizens are easy to manipulate?

The dulling effect of shallow tv-programmes

There is an excess of programmes in the soap, show, quiz and make-over (make me more beautiful) genres. Moreover there is a superabundant offer of stupid advertisement publicity, to my great annoyance. There used to be a time where I could have used an extra pair of hands to zap from one good film to the other. A good, compelling film for me covers a social theme and offers lively interaction between the actors in which romance plays an important role. Good films such as *Dancing with Wolves, The House of the Spirits* and *The Unbearable Lightness of Being* make you forget about the world for about 90 minutes. Good films open your mind, touch your heart and make you think. It has been proved that the body releases endorphins ('feel good' hormones) while watching a good film. I really regret that I hardly see a good film on the Dutch television and consider all this coarsening and superficiality as a decline of our civilization. According to Gary Zukav, women feel washed-out by their busy, overburdened lives and 70% of the American women don't feel any passion anymore. That may explain the success of films including *Under the Tuscan Sun* and *Eat, Pray, Love,* where women, who seem to have everything they desire, start looking for meaning and inspiration and their first stop on this journey is Italy, because 'amore e mangiare' is the Italian way of life in a setting of the sun-drenched Tuscan landscape or the cultural wealth of Rome. But not everyone has the courage or money to head to the other side of the world.

According to Clarissa Pinkola Estés, author of the book *Women Who Run With the Wolves: Myths and Stories of the Wild Woman Archetype,* women with a starving soul ache for anything that might spark their lives. They run the risk of abandoning themselves to excesses like alcohol, drugs and unhappy love affairs.

Being the powerful medium it is, television should offer more programmes that help us to lead a healthy and happy life and help parents to educate their children in the right way.

Parents and teachers have no idea of the negative impact of their disapproval behaviour; like 'You are good for nothing', etc.

I HAVE A MESSAGE FOR ALL PARENTS AND TEACHERS: BE AWARE OF THE IMPACT OF WHAT YOU SAY

For instance: Don't say you are a bad boy, but this is bad behaviour and explain why. It can be very helpful to teach the children empathy and compassion on the basis of an exercise, where the teaser takes the place of the victim of this teasing and has to feel what it means.

MASTER YOUR MIND!

REVEAL YOUR SUB-PERSONALITIES

Until the moment we truly know ourselves, we find ourselves in the unpleasant position of being a passenger in our own car of life (or worse, being trapped in the trunk) while our sub-personalities are taking turns driving it.

Hal Stone and Sidra Winkelman wrote a very valuable book together: *Embracing Ourselves*. They very clearly describe the situation most of us are in, within in the current society.

The development of our sub-personalities

Each and every baby comes into this world with its own genetic make-up and a special, unique essence. Stone & Winkelman call this the essence level of the newborn. I would rather call it the level of the True Self. No other creature is as defenseless as a newborn baby, totally dependent on its parents for food and nurturing love. In each culture there is a common agreement about desirable and undesirable behavior.

During the education desirable behavior will be rewarded and undesirable behavior will be punished. As a result certain parts of us will be stronger and other parts will be weaker. We gradually loose contact with our True Self during this process and we start developing all kinds of sub-personalities in order to survive in our complex, industrialized society. We are no longer the creators of our lives.

Instead we have become 'pawns on a chessboard', servants of market laws and profit seeking, and get trapped in possessiveness and greed. We have forgotten who we really are and what we really want. Our minds rule and we don't have enough connection with our hearts.

In our western culture there are four sub-personalities (energy patterns) which dominate our lives.

The pusher is always chasing us up to work harder and doesn't allow us to relax.

The perfectionist want us to do everything perfectly might and **the critic** makes us always clear that we are not good enough.

On top of that is a fourth sub-personality that dominates the life of women. That type of women ignore their own needs in order to be able to offer a helping hand.

It's time for women to upgrade their self-image and to become aware of the incredible amount of work they're carrying out. Raising children is the most important job in the world!

There is only one way to liberate yourself from identification with your sub-personalities: the way to awareness. The key is to step out of the world of your sub-personalities and observe them and their behaviour from a distance.

As soon as you start working with your sub-personalities, a fascinating process begins. And your efforts will be increasingly rewarded.

You will discover that each step out of the world of your sub-personalities is a step into the world of your True Self. In other words; the more you liberate yourself from the identification with your sub-personalities, the more you will experience your True Self.

There is another effective way to restore the contact with your True Self.

Meditation is a very powerful and effective way to get to know your True Self. The self that you were born with. It helps you to fully direct your attention inward.

This deactivates your common thinking patterns and opens your intuitive channel, allowing you to connect to your inner being.

In addition, meditation has a very positive impact on your body and mind.

Regular meditation reinforces our immune system, helps us to relax in a natural way and to achieve a better balance, which is so much better that taking in all those tranquillizers. I'm pretty sure no other activity on earth leads to as many benefits as meditating does!

The snowball effect will do its work; the further you get in the awareness process, the faster the snowball will roll since the positive effects will increasingly reinforce each other. Based on my own experience, I can assure you how incredibly good it feels to embrace your True Self. It provides you with a sense of faith in your destiny, inner peace, joy, gratitude and it makes you feel connected to your fellow human beings, animals and nature. Your True Self grants you a still point in the midst of all the noise you are surrounded by. What's more, it gives you the feeling you are the creator of your own life; you drive your own car of life towards the destinations you have chosen yourself. Your sub-personalities are your passengers and will carry out the commands you give them in order to reach those destinations.

It's very important that parents help their children develop self-esteem and stimulate their intuition and creativity. You can only truly love another person if you truly love yourself and you can only take good care of our planet if you are able to take good care of yourself. So there is a lot of work to be done! And you can start right now!

First of all you must be aware of the fact that the climate crisis is our greatest threat.

There is an enormous lack of awareness of the dangers of climate change among large sections of the population.

This book offers you a way out of the global crisis. It provides you with world-wide research results regarding the food and lifestyle that keep you healthy and slim, and universal wisdom regarding the conditions for profound happiness. It shows you solutions for our present problems and how we can build a sustainable economy together, while respecting nature and gives you many inspiring examples of people who are working already to create a better world.

This path is based on three pillars:

- **awareness**
- **insight**
- **action**

The insight that humans are predestined to be lovingly connected to themselves, their fellow human beings and nature, automatically leads to the will to realize a happy and healthy future.

IT'S A MATTER OF MAKING THE RIGHT CHOICES…

The choices we make today, determine our future

So don't wait any longer

Wake up and do everything you can do to save our planet

Together we are strong to create a better future!

A HEALTHY LIFE IS A DAILY JOY

The way people treat themselves is striking. They treat their car as if it were a sacred cow and themselves as the neglected calf.

Everything has to be sacrificed for this number one status symbol and we spend lots of money to buy and maintain our inanimate 'pet'. How differently do we treat our own bodies; our bodies are rushed, abused and stuffed with unwholesome food and stimulating products like tobacco, alcohol and other drugs.

Our so called health is not what it appears to be! Many people think they are healthy since they can't actually see the damage done. However, this so called state of health is not real.

The damage done to your body as a result of an unnatural, stressful lifestyle can be considered a dangerous cumulative effect. Ever more toxins are added until the pressure becomes too high and your body breaks down. If you're lucky, you're able to fix the damage. If not, you won't survive. When you start noticing the consequences of this damage and you suffer from chronic fatigue or worse, from diabetes, or a heart attack, your whole world will fall into pieces and you are forced to become aware of your lifestyle and eating habits.

Our unhealthy lifestyle creates diseases of affluence.

We have developed an unhealthy lifestyle with too much tension and stress, and an unhealthy diet consisting of too much sugar, refined white flour and saturated fats.

This lifestyle causes a whole range of so-called diseases of affluence like cancer, diabetes, cardiovascular disease and obesity. The costs for health-care increase worldwide, and become too expensive.

There is one effective way to limit these costs: knowledge of healthy food and respect for nature must become part of the school curriculum.

It is easy to stay healthy and slim your whole life long. Mother Nature offers us everything we need: whole grains, seas full of fish, wild animals, and lots of edible plants, fruits and seeds. And to sweeten our food there's honey, maple syrup and concentrated fruit syrup.

But instead of being grateful for these gifts that keep us healthy our food is refined so much, that only a little of the original nutritional value is left in them.

One of the biggest mistakes is throwing away the precious 'coat' of the grain, the husk. It contains badly needed valuable fibers and minerals.

Another mistake is using too much sugar instead of natural sweeteners. Their high carbohydrate levels weaken our immune system, make us fat, disturb our intestinal flora and attribute to developing hypoglycemia and diabetes.

Recent scientific studies have also shown that sugar can damage our proteins through a process of glycation, resulting in a sort of cellular also waste production in our cells, causing premature ageing.

ALL YOU HAVE TO KNOW TO STAY HEALTHY AND SLIM

Many people think a healthy lifestyle demands a great effort. I see overweight people struggling with diets that are not helpful at all because of their yoyo-effect. Overweight is an increasingly common problem. About half of the people living in the industrialised countries are overweight. This problem will become bigger and bigger, unless we will drastically change our eating habits. So I recommend you not to follow a strict diet; simply start eating natural food.

All sorts of international research (including the Oxford-Peking research and the Okinawa study) reveal the best ingredients for optimal health. The Okinawa inhabitants, who grow very old without suffering from any age-related diseases, turn out to have the optimal balance between omega 3 and 6. This balance also helps to stay mentally balanced and helps ADHD children to calm down.

In Okinawa, they eat a lot of fresh vegetables and soy products. They effortlessly reach the age of 90. Also many centenarians in Okinawa still live an active life since our Western age related diseases hardly exist there.

Dan Buettner did thorough research on the secret of these people and found out it involves a combination of several factors, including a healthy diet, sufficient outdoor exercise, proper social contacts, commitment to a life goal and a sunny climate (a mood booster and provider of free vitamin D). Okinawa is part of the so called Blue Zones, also located in Sardinia (Italy), where the Melis family ended up in the Guinness Book of Records because of holding the record of the amount of centenarians. Also the Greek Island of Ikaria is part of the Blue Zones.

However, don't be mistaken by thinking these are the only areas to be safeguarded from cancer, cardiovascular diseases and Alzheimer.

In the USA they have started an interesting project: in 14 cities they imitated the conditions of the Blue Zones and the positive results have already been measured.

In one of these cities, health costs have already been reduced with 40%.

AVOID FATAL FATS AND USE VITAL FATS

According to the Belgium writer Jo Wijckmans, whose book *Gezond van binnen, van buiten mooi* (which means 'Healthy On The Inside, Beautiful On The Outside') became a bestseller, a low-fat diet is not healthy. A diet rich in good essential fatty acids (vital fats) is essential to fight being overweight.

Top experts are getting more and more convinced of the fact that one of the most effective tools to fight obese are oils rich in ALA (Alpha-Linolenic Acid) such as flaxseed (linseed) oil, chia oil, echium oil and perilla oil. In addition, the intake of Gamma LinolecAcid (an omega 6 fatty acid) is very important for our health. GLA is found in evening primrose oil and borage oil (M.F.). If you combine this with fish oil (an omega 3 fatty acid) rich in DHA and a diet rich in fibres, you are doing everything you need for perfect weight control and optimal health.

On top of this, the healthy oils will protect you against cardiovascular diseases, heart attacks and other degenerative diseases. Wijckmans also points out that unhealthy transfats are not just contained by margarine but by almost all refined food products in our supermarkets, including pan-fried and deep-fried dishes, industrial sponge cakes, waffles, cookies, crackers, peanut butter, crisps, pizza's etc.

Trans-fats and saturated fats	Polyunsaturated fatty acids
<ul><li>Increase the risk of cancer Increase the risk of a heart attack or stroke</li><li>Block our arteries</li><li>Have a negative effect on our brain function</li><li>Cause depressions</li><li>Damage the immune system</li><li>Aggravate inflammations etc.</li></ul>	<ul><li>Decrease the risk of cancer</li><li>Provide protection against a heart attack/stroke</li><li>Clean our arteries</li><li>Improve our brain function</li><li>Reduce depressions Strengthen our immune system Reduce</li><li>inflammations etc.</li></ul>

The Dutch company called Witsenburg with its own brand 'Omega & More', states that transfats and saturated fats are extremely unhealthy and polyunsaturated fatty acids add to our health in a very positive way.

This company recommends us to deepfry as little as possible and to replace the oil wherever we can. They suggest to use coconut oil for baking and roasting. I use a thin layer of refined olive oil and eventually absorb the fat with a kitchen paper towel. I use plenty of cold-pressed olive oil for cabbage salads. In addition, I use other vital fats including linseed oil, evening primrose oil and borage oil to help me keep healthy and slim. My weight hasn't changed in 40 years! I am never tired and I can stay up all night.

If you start eating in a wholesome, unprocessed, organic way and start exercising consciously and focused, your condition will improve, your energy level will raise and you will automatically loose weight.

A healthy diet contains several kinds of whole wheat grains, a small amount of <u>organic</u> meat, a little beef, fish (be careful with farmed fish; they are often given antibiotics) and soy products (including tofu) on a regular basis. Eat lots of legumes, lots of fresh vegetables and fruit, nuts and seeds (especially linseed), a little salt (preferably sea salt or Himalayan salt).

Variation and alternation are important. Multigrain Bread is better than bread of one cereal. Exchange whole grain rice with buckwheat, quinoa, etc! Eat regular legumes and in between potatoes (especially sweet potatoes!)

Finally and very important:

Eat no sugar or as little sugar as possible. Use malt syrup, rice syrup, stevia or, in moderation, cold extracted honey or maple syrup to replace sugar.

Drink lots of water and green tea. It's better for you to curb your meat consumption anyway (The World Health Organisation research has shown that regularly eating processed meat increases the risk of cancer). On the contrary the consumption of soy products decreases the risk of hormone related cancer, like breast cancer or prostate cancer because soy contains fyto-oestrogens with the precious isoflavons. The consumption of fresh fruit (specially the red and black like black berries, cherries and blue grapes) also gives us a good protection.

Besides that, eating too much meat is bad for our climate and for the worldwide food supply. Specially cattle-breeding with cows contributes to global warming by methane emissions. Moreover to produce **one** kilogram beef meat, a cow needs to eat **seven** times as much vegetable food and with this kind of food we can save the lives of the people on earth that are starving from hunger.

Restrict your dairy intake as well, except for yoghurt, containing the bifido bacterium lactis which contributes to healthy gut flora. Excessive intake of triglycerides, also called the fatal fat, is one of the risk factors for cardiovascular disease, and contributes to acidic build-up in our bodies which may cause rheumatic conditions. So to fight acidic build-up you need to eat lots of fresh fruit and vegetables.

THE GREAT VALUE OF FRESH ORGANIC VEGETABLES AND FRUIT

Prof. Dr. Defares informs us of the great importance of fresh vegetables and fruit, and advises us to eat 400 grams per day as prevention against cancer.

Broccoli and other vegetables of the **Brassica** family are a good source of, for example, the substance **sulforaphane**, which can protect us against cancer. Onions and garlic contain the substance **allylsulphide**, which has the ability to detoxify carcinogens (substances which play a role in the onset of cancer). Tomatoes are rich in lycopene. This valuable substance can slow down the damaging oxidation process in our cells, and in high concentrations is even believed to delay the onset of cancer.

Furthermore, large-scale international research led by Prof. Kok (Wageningen) indicates that people who eat large amounts of vegetables and fruit have a greatly reduced risk of suffering a heart attack.

Ruud Nieuwenhuis was director of the Foundation for Orthomolecular Education.

(In orthomolecular medicine an optimal biochemical environment is created by means of the intake of optimal food and dietary supplements, whereby cellular restoration processes are given the best opportunity to thrive).

He has written five books, and in his extensive *Handbook of Vitamins and Self-Care* he gives the following advice with regard to the eating of vegetables:

"Use food that has been processed as little as possible, during both cultivation and preparation. At least one third of the main daily meal should consist of raw vegetables. Raw vegetables provide the most enzymes and other micronutrients. They are unprocessed food, and only unprocessed food is natural food. Begin your meal with them." (Micronutrients are vitamins, minerals and trace elements that perform many essential functions in our bodies).

Only organic food contains all micronutrients that provide us with the valuable building material we need to stay healthy. The average supermarket food has a very poor nutritional value as a result of the use of fertilizers, pesticides, chemical additives and gamma rays. In addition, this kind of food contains too much sugar, salt and fatal fats. All of this results in a serious vitamin and mineral deficiency, which leads to a poor physical condition, to being overweight and eventually to typical western diseases, such as cardiovascular disease and diabetes.

Nieuwenhuis also highlights another important motive for eating plenty of vegetables and fruit: it contributes to the correct regulation of acidity levels throughout the body.

The German acid/alkali expert Ragnar Berg gives the following advice:

"Eat five to seven times the amount (by weight) of vegetables and fruit as all other foodstuff put together. This advice is based on the principle that vegetable-based food contains a surplus of alkalis, whereas animal-based food has an overall acidifying effect. Moreover, every day a portion of your vegetables should be eaten raw".

When you follow this advice, then 80% of your food should be of a generally alkaline nature, resulting in your bodily tissues maintaining their correct pH-level.

This is of great importance to our health, because an incorrect PH-level slows down enzyme activity.

In the year 2000 I worked intensively alongside Ruud Nieuwenhuis and I learned a great deal from him. Together we drafted a Press release for a healthy New Year, with valuable advice in the field of nutrition and supplementary vitamins and minerals.

Sadly, this pioneer has since died but I still regularly consult his excellent books.

SUGAR AND STRESS ARE THE CAUSES OF NEW DISEASES OF AFFLUENCE

First, we need to realise that basically all our diseases are related to our unhealthy lifestyle in the industrialised countries. The amount of people suffering from diseases of affluence including being overweight, cardiovascular diseases, cancer and diabetes, was much smaller before the Industrial Revolution. However, a new category of so-called new diseases of affluence hitting a growing amount of people has come along.

Examples are systemic candidiasis, hypoglycaemia and chronic fatigue syndrome. Over 10% of the population in the industrialised countries suffer from these diseases and this percentage is still growing at an alarming pace.

SYSTEMIC CANDIDA

Candida albicans is a yeast like fungus, usually Y-shaped and residing in the body (including the intestines) in relatively small amounts.

However, affected by an unhealthy diet containing sugar and white flour products, antibiotics and too much stress, the balance of the intestinal flora is disturbed.

It is a well-known fact that antibiotics (especially broad spectrum antibiotics) kill both the good bacteria as well as the bad ones. This deactivates the lactobacillus acidophilus, the name of the bacteria that usually controls the candida.

We know that the candida yeast cell lives of sugar (amongst others), which makes it easy to understand that consuming large amounts of refined sugar in combination with the use of antibiotics can result in an explosive growth of candida.

But also other factors, including a long lasting unwholesome diet, long term negative stressful situations, environmental pollution, post-viral syndromes and the use of cortisone preparations can cause systemic candidiasis.

In addition, because of all these negative conditions, the controllable Y-shaped yeast like fungus turns into a malignant M-shaped fungus. This M-shape has developed cords which can infiltrate into the blood stream via damaged areas in the intestine wall.

The results are disastrous because in this form the candida is hardly destructible by the immune system. To top it all off, all kinds of toxins are being secreted, free to flow through the whole body via the veins.

When this stage is reached, the condition is called a systemic candidiasis infection, capable of causing many different symptoms, including chronic fatigue, digestive disorders, muscular pain, chronic infections, impotence and/or lack of libido and allergies.

Psychic symptoms include: anxieties, mood swings, crying fits and depressions.

In time, the immune system will be entirely disordered, making the patient prone to very severe diseases like multiple sclerosis, arthritis and cancer. In addition, a weakened immune system results in a disordered hormone balance, allowing another severe disease to easily find its way into the body; hypoglycaemia.

I will get back to this subject in detail later. Your regular family doctor will not be able to treat systemic candidiasis since, in general, he or she is not familiar enough with this infection.

I would recommend Candida patients to visit an orthomolecular expert for a 'live blood analysis' to diagnose a systemic candidiasis infection. In addition, research techniques like the Vega Test or, even better, the Mora Test (part of bio-resonance therapy) can determine the level of damage that has been done.

The candida treatment includes four steps:

1. **Killing the candida fungus**
2. **Boosting the immune system**
3. **Restoring digestive health**

4. **A strict sugar, yeast, fungus and refined cereal
   free diet**

HYPOGLYCAEMIA

We already discussed the risk of a disordered hormone balance caused by a weakened immune system. This imbalance clears the path for the hypoglycaemia syndrome to enter the body. Hypoglycaemia is a physical condition where the pancreas works too hard because of the sugar level in one's diet being too high. This results in low blood glucose which continuously pushes the adrenal glands to (amongst others) produce more adrenaline to compensate the low glucose level. The adrenal gland is a stress organ designed to bring the body in a state of alert in cases of acute emergency, allowing someone to, for instance, escape as fast as he can from a burning house. This state of alert is created by elevating the blood sugar level, providing the body with the necessary energy to take action.

Only few people realise that chronic stress situations including overload, irritation, anger and hate, cause similar symptoms resulting in a continuously elevated blood sugar level.

This condition forces the pancreas to continuously produce extra insulin in order to compensate the high blood sugar level.

This proves that hypoglycaemia is clearly related to our western way of life, caused by eating refined foods (white flour products and sugar) and too much stress.

Also stimulants like tobacco and alcohol can be a part of the cause of hypoglycaemia. In nature, there is no such thing as fast carbohydrates, only complex, slowly processed carbohydrates.

Therefore, our bodies are not designed to process simple, fast carbohydrates from refined modern food products. Time after time again, they force the pancreas to suddenly go in overdrive from a rest position.

In time, the thermo-regulator breaks down which leads to a continuous overproduction of insulin, resulting in a low blood sugar. This is why hypoglycaemia is also called hyperinsulinism.

This physical condition results in all kinds of serious complaints including chronic fatigue, lack of concentration (confusion), headaches, dizziness, muscle pain, palpitations, memory problems, shivering and excessive sweating. On top of this, the brains are lacking glucose which can cause severe psychic problems including anxiety, phobias, irritation, aggression, nervousness and depressions.

Eventually, hypoglycaemia can lead to diabetes, that's why this condition is by no means harmless.

The hypoglycaemia treatment consists of the following four steps:

1. **A diet free of sugar, refined cereals and coffee;**
2. **Food supplements consisting of vitamins and minerals (especially chrome);**
3. **Avoiding stress or learning how to deal with stress;**
4. **Sufficient exercise.**

EFFECTIVE REMEDIES: TO COMBAT AGE-RELATED AILMENTS

People who are consuming mainly supermarket food should be taking natural vitamin and mineral supplements.

Avoid synthetic products because they are not well assimilated in our body.

As we grow older, it's even more important to take extra vitamins and minerals. Our body is a complex machine and while we're ageing, certain cogs will start to break down which makes our functions deteriorate.

If we compensate the deficiency of certain materials in a natural way by taking food supplements, our bodies stay healthy and vital for much longer.

I am a great advocate of the use of extra vitamins, minerals and nutritional supplements, due to the fact that food bought in the average supermarket is so deficient.

According to Ruud Nieuwenhuis, research has shown that shortages of essential vitamins, minerals and trace elements in the diet inevitably lead to health problems in the form of extensive loss of condition and the onset of cardiovascular diseases and cancer.

In this respect he draws our attention to the fact that these modern sicknesses also play a large part in cell degeneration caused by the action of so-called 'free radicals'. These are aggressive oxygen ions that arise from the complex process of oxygen uptake and energy release in our bodily cells. This may sound alarming, but there are actually enzymes at work during this whole process which break down and remove these free radicals.

However, the influence of such varied factors as deficient foodstuffs (in particular the presence in our food of synthetic additives, the so-called 'E-numbers'), environmental pollution, stress, smoking, too much alcohol and excessive sunbathing results in the accumulation of too many free radicals for our bodies to deal with.

Furthermore, the protective action of enzymes decreases with the ageing process.

It is therefore particularly important for older people to regularly take a naturally-based antioxidant complex of a good brand, for example Solgar. This company issues beneficial inserts and leaflets with information about their products.

- In order to fight joint problems such as arthrosis, natural remedies like glucosamine and chondroitin, m.s.m., silica and bamboo help improve the production and function of cartilage cells.
- Supplements such as folic acid, vitamin E, gingko biloba, coenzim Q10 alpha-Lipoic acid and vitamin B12 are great when fighting deterioration of our mental health. Research shows that people over 60 all have a vitamin B12 deficiency because the levels of a certain protein produced in the stomach that helps absorbing this vitamin are decreasing. A deficiency may result in memory problems, dementia and Alzheimer. That is why people over 60 are recommended to take vitamin B12 supplements on a daily basis (source: Carper, 'Your Miracle Brain).
- Research showed that also the intake of curcuma helps fighting mental deterioration. In countries where large amounts of curcuma are consumed, far less people suffer from this disease.
- A large group of people starting from middle age has to contend with varicose veins, tired legs and cramps. It is important that our foods contains enough anti-oxidants to

protect artery walls. Especially vitamin C, Bioflavonoids and OPC's play an important role. You will find them in (forest) berries, citrus fruits, onions, garlic and ginger and green tea. Because our modern diet contains too little anti-oxidants. I recommend especially people in middle age to take one gram of natural vitamin C and an OPC-complex which contains, among other things, grape seeds and pine nuts. Also the extract horse chestnut (aesculus hippocastanum) helps to keep blood vessels in healthy condition.

- For women who have entered menopause, natural hormone preparations like hormone creams can be very beneficial. Oprah Winfrey has pointed this out in her shows several times. Women on her show talked about their complaints as a result of a hormonal imbalance. The symptoms included depressed feelings, fatigue, insomnia etc. After using the cream, these women started to feel much better. You may want to carry out a DIY test to measure your hormonal (im-)balance. You can also consider visiting a centre for hormone related complaints. I have been using a natural progesterone cream developed by the well-known dr. John Lee.

Make sure not to be misguided by incorrect information aiming to discredit the importance of wholesome, organic food, food supplements in order to fight age related diseases, and the benefits of naturopathy. There are forces infiltrating the media since they have an interest in us being sick.

THE GOVERNMENT SHOULD BE FAR MORE COMMITTED TO A HEALTH ENCOURAGING POLICY

Information on healthy food should be part of the curriculum of each and every school. Supermarkets should be forced to sell more healthy food without any chemical flavourings and colourings and fatal fats, that contains far less sugar and salt. The same goes for school canteens! Currently, everything is depending on free market forces and supermarket chains claim they are not able to change their policy because it will make them loose customers to other supermarkets. Consumers should inform themselves more on the huge risks of the large-scale food production, and put pressure on supermarkets and the government to change their policy.

Exercise regularly to stay healthy

To people who want to avoid being overweight, I recommend to act as soon as you put on a few kilos by introducing a healthy diet and work-outs into your daily life. That way, it'll be so much easier to loose these extra kilos.

Regular exercise, in addition to a varied, wholesome and organic diet, is a crucial aspect for a healthy lifestyle. Ever since the Industrial Revolution, we mainly spend our lives sitting inside. Our working lives in offices and factories, where we spend an average 8 hours a day sitting or standing up carrying out monotonous work, don't give our body the exercise it needs. After work we rush home by car, bus or train (only a small percentage by bike) where we have dinner and sit on the settee for hours to watch television or stare at our computers. Our exercise is limited to the weekends, which is way too little to stay healthy, slim and fit. Children spend less playing outside and more and more time playing computer games.

Half of the people living in industrialized countries are overweight and this will only get worse unless we change our lifestyles.

You will not give your body enough exercise unless you integrate it in your daily life

There are plenty of ways to exercise, individually or in a group. You can play a sport, go hiking, running, dancing or swimming, go to the gym or work in the garden. Whatever you do it's important to make it an integral part of your daily schedule. You will increasingly enjoy doing it since your health will improve and energy levels will increase and also mentally you will feel much better!

As a social scientist, I have been committed to research into the conditions for a healthy and happy life for 48 years. In addition, I am an expert by experience. I was raised with white bread topped with lots of sugar and chocolate sprinkles, and overcooked dinners. I used to be ill frequently when I was a little girl. I was suffering from the flue, ear infections and once I suffered from meningitis.

As soon as I left home, I started to eat only organic food. Since then, I hardly ever became ill and I always stayed slim. The reason for my burnout around my forties was a result of my overloaded life. On top of the work I already did, I was invited to start a totally new project which involved working in a prison and giving training to the police and criminal investigators. In my sixties, I did suffer from Lyme disease caused by a tick bite. Fortunately, I overcame Lyme disease by a combination of antibiotics and the ingenious bio-resonance therapy.

As a highly sensitive person, I suffered a lot since I used to join people and animals in their suffering instead of empathising with them. In addition, I raised a child suffering from severe diabetes and built a career as a teacher and psychotherapist at the same time. Besides this, I have frequently participated in protests in order to fight social injustice and helped people and animals in need whenever and wherever I could. So to me it's very clear that without organic food, additional vitamins and food supplements to improve age-related diseases and limitations, naturopathy and my decision to always live in the countryside in order to benefit from the healing powers of nature, I would probably have passed away years ago.

BURNOUT: A CAREFUL, ACCURATE DIAGNOSIS IS THE KEY TO HEALING

More and more people in the industrial society (also very young people) are getting burned out. If you suffer from a burnout it is very important to quiet down and take time to recover.

Follow the diet advise I gave in this chapter, take care of enough bodily exercise and take restorative remedies like ginger, bee-pollen or ginseng. You can also take medicinal herbs to create more energy like Rhodiola rosea, Schisandria chinensis, Withania somnifera or to strengthen your nervous system: Scutellaria baicalensis.

If you don't recover it is possible that you suffer from Systemic Candisiasis, Hypoglycemia and you can cure yourself with the instructions in this chapter.

But it is also possible that you suffer from a so called Post-viral-syndrom (PVS) for instance that you don't recover after a virus infection. This happened to me and it became clear that this was caused by the Epstein-Barr virus that has a negative effect on the liver.

Finally it is possible that you suffer from the disease of Lyme, caused by a tick bite or that you suffer from the negative effect of an old amalgam-filling in your mouth and in that case you have to ask your dentist to remove them.

When I was burned out for the second time, I suffered from both causes and I remember how awful I felt: I walked with leaden feet and cottonwool in my head.

This general view of the causes of burn out makes clear that a good diagnosis is the key to a good healing.

In Holland the regular medical science is not able to diagnose the disease of Lyme and to give you right treatment. They give you only an antibiotic cure and if it does not help, Dutch patients recourse to Germany where the best diagnosis is possible because the Bio-resonance method is very developed. If this method is not available where you live, there also other methods like the Vega-test, Live-blood-analysis, touch-for-health, etc.

THE EFFECTIVE RESULTS FROM NATUROPATHIC REMEDIES

If you become ill, always look for natural remedies like phytotherapy, homeopathy, gemmotherapy etc., first. And don't forget valuable treatment methods like acupuncture and the impressive bio-resonance therapy.

Phytotherapy is centuries old

The herbal medicine is as old as the world itself. As in earlier times women went into the forest to look for medicinal plants and herbs, and by doing so they actually laid the foundation of medicine.

These herbal medicine, which is now also known as phytotherapy, is not to be confused with homeopathy, which also works with a large number of preparations out of the plant world, but in the form of highly diluted solutions. Also, homeopathy doesn't confine itself to just plants, but it also makes use of animal products and minerals. (For example: Lachesis of A. Vogel, is prepared from snake venom).

During the last century, many herb gardens in monasteries disappeared, and growing herbs was taken over by pharmacists.

Only in a later stage medicine introduced all kinds of synthetic compounds.

I have noticed that the pharmaceutical lobby is increasingly trying to damage the reputation of naturopathy. It has already succeeded in limiting the availability of the vast supply of homeopathic supplements in a drastic way by demanding expensive patents. I am seriously irritated by these bad practices since I truly benefited from natural remedies. These don't result in any negative side effects. Sometimes, allopathic medication is worse than the disease itself because of the negative side effects.

What's more, fake medication is being brought on the market, produced in countries including China. Finally, as a result of the health care market conditions, doctors tend to subscribe cheaper medication. In Holland, doctors are even rewarded with a bonus from the health insurance companies if they adjust to this tendency.

Naturopathy is on the up and this development cannot be stopped, despite the negative publicity coming from conventional medicine and the big pharmaceutical industries. Obviously they feel threatened and want to protect their major financial interests.

In addition, natural remedies are freely available in most drugstores, pharmacies and organic shops. At home, I created my own private pharmacy since I like to manage my own health as much as I can. In case I become ill in the middle of the night, I don't have to wake up anyone. I am able to take action myself. My thirty years of experience with phytotherapy and homeopathy have made me very enthusiastic about their results. Besides helping myself, I was also able to help family and friends, and even my pets, with it!

I have never been against conventional medicine but in my opinion conventional and naturopathy should be joining forces.

I greatly admire surgeons carrying out lifesaving and incredibly detailed operations.

They have saved the life of my son Cyril, who has been suffering from juvenile diabetes since he was ten, by giving him a new crystalline lens, and a donor kidney and pancreas.

Speaking of miracles:

Six year ago, my son's condition was very bad. His kidneys were so weak, he needed dialysis. He was on the waiting list for a double organ donation but he had to wait a long time before it was his turn. I was so desperate I started saying the rosary. I asked my friends and family to pray with me and guess what? After a while, he was offered a kidney and pancreas twice in one week. Although it was a challenging operation, he was able to go home after a month already.

Unfortunately, Cyril died totally unexpectedly in October 2016 because of a cerebral hemorrhage. I was deeply shocked and it took me a long period of mourning because he was not only my dear son, but also a very dear and wise friend.

And the next poem he wrote for me is a testimony of his wisdom.

You are one of a kind,
there is no other!
You are a good and fine person
with a great passion and power
You are my mother
and I love you
Things that happened in the past,
Let's forget them
and look for the future
and make the best of it!

Your son Cyril xxx

This beautiful fragment gives rise to an important advice: Express your love and appreciation for your dear ones!

Many people remain with guilt feelings when somebody dies unexpectedly and it is not possible anymore.

PERSONAL POSITIVE EXPERIENCE WITH NATURAL REMEDIES

During my whole life, I have always looked for natural remedies coming from naturopathy and I successfully cured all my diseases. I only used antibiotics when really necessary but never without using probiotics at the same time in order to build up my natural flora again. Today, I feel better than ever and I never feel tired. My energy level is so high; I can easily work all night.

I will give you three examples of how natural remedies worked for me:

The first example happened eighteen years ago: In spring 1998, I took the initiative to open up a gallery for visual arts. Key theme was: "Art mediation service for women". The gallery had to be sanded and painted and I, being the wayward woman that I am, didn't want to wait for my boyfriend to come home and help me in the weekend.

So I hired two heavy sanding machines and started sanding pitched roof walls, exceeding the limits of my physical power. After days of sanding, my right arm and shoulder started aching and I ended up with a tennis elbow and a bursitis.

I tried everything to heal my arm and shoulder: physiotherapy, injections etc. The result was a cured tennis elbow but a chronic bursitis. It became worse and worse and in autumn 1998, I was no longer able to write. This condition lasted for several months. Then (and I don't know why I hadn't thought of it before) I decided to visit my homeopathic doctor. She prescribed two remedies: Ruta (Graveolens) D6 and Ferrum Metallicum D6. Within no time a miracle happened: the pain disappeared and never came back. I did a happy dance, finally I could go back to writing!

The second example took place far from home. While travelling by train or boat, I always seem to be confronted with people that are groaning with pain at night. Horrible for those people, but not very nice for me either. Continuously being disturbed while trying to get some sleep is exhausting.

But look who we have here: 'Florence Nightingale' selecting the right medicine from her private homeopathic travel kit and inside there is always a remedy to relieve the pain.

Once, I was on a Greek island hopping journey and a woman in our cabin was screaming with pain. She was suffering from a cystitis and urged me to look for a doctor on board. I offered her Cantharis D6 which she rejected since nothing had ever cured her cystitis before, as she assured me. I was able to convince her to give it a try anyway. Within no time the pain disappeared and she was able to sleep. However, in case of cystitis, make sure to get a diagnose from your doctor through a urine test. Also have your urine tested after your homeopathic treatment. Make sure to drink a lot, solidago tea for instance. The symptoms of an overactive bladder are similar to those of cystitis, however they need to be treated differently.

The third example shows the very positive experience I have had with fresh ginger root. In the year 2000, my hearing suddenly started to get worse quickly. I never discovered the cause of it but within no time I could no longer answer the phone since I wasn't able to hear what the caller was saying. I made an appointment with a nose throat and ear specialist. To my astonishment, I didn't even hear my own name being called out through the intercom. The specialist wanted to do a minor operation but that didn't feel right for me. Instead, I contacted a macrobiotic centre in Antwerp. They advised me to make a tea of rasped ginger root and to dip a tea towel in hot ginger root water, squeeze the water out, fold it and put it around my head behind my ears, as a bow. Also, I had to eat loads of radish sprinkled with tamari. Within a few days my hearing went back to normal (and never got worse again). I was over the moon since a hearing problem can make you feel very isolated. Since that time, I understood what somebody with a hearing problem must feel like.

Finally, natural remedies helped me to heal the dramatic results of Lyme disease. The number of victims of this disease, caused by a tick bite, is growing. Lyme can completely destroy people by deactivating brain functions, resulting in paralysis.

I was suffering from heart and brain failure and lost control over my life.

I suffered from a heart rhythm disturbance. On top of that my heartbeat was often much to low and went down to 40, and my blood pressures was much too high and went up to 180. Sometimes I could not sleep and became so restless that I started to walk in my garden at 3 o'clock at night. My cardiologist prescribed Tambocor but I preferred to try first natural remedies. I started to use crataegus-complex, which is made out of the hawthorn tree. This is a wonderful remedy.

On top of that I used L-carnitine, taurine and bio quinon (Q10) to reinforce my heart. With this cocktail (which I still use every day) I managed to cure my heart problems, but I was not able to cure my brain failure. That's why I had to travel to Holland in the middle of winter, where the best bio-resonance therapist has his practice.

He is also a dear friend and is incredible multilateral.

He has a large test box containing many ampoules that can be used to determine whether or not you've got Lyme disease, and to diagnose the Lyme variant.

I was suffering from two co-infections: Ehrlichia and Silicea and this magnificent bio-resonance device is capable of producing the right remedy, which enabled me to recover step by step. One day, my therapist said to me: 'It's time to open a bottle of champagne, because we did it!'

For that, I will be eternally grateful to him. The reason for this detailed story is the small amount of information that is available on the right treatment. The ticks keep on muting, creating more and more Lyme variants that are increasingly difficult to treat. Conventional medicine only prescribes antibiotics. Very often, these antibiotics don't cure the disease and weaken the immune system at the same time. That is why I recommend you to always use probiotics when using anti-biotics. If the patient returns to his doctor with the same symptoms, there is no further treatment available.

That is why many Dutch patients go to Germany for their treatment since in that country bio-resonance therapy is in a far more developed stage. In general, people are poorly informed on Lyme disease and the reactions of some female friends were very painful for me: 'Oh, have you got Lyme disease? It seems as if there is always something wrong with you!' and 'Oh, are you scared? I thought you were a strong woman!'

I remember being in an early stage of the disease and losing my consciousness three times. Once, in Spain, I woke up in an unfamiliar bed, seeing a man I had never seen before, sitting on a chair staring at me. I was startled and ran outside.

After an experience like this, you cannot stop yourself from being scared.

However, besides the negative reactions, also heart-warming reactions came my way, like that time I caused a collision. I crashed into the back of a car of a family who were on their way to France for their holiday.

I felt horrible and apologised immediately: 'I'm so sorry, I've got Lyme disease and I wasn't paying attention'.

I expected them to be furious but I saw a woman looking at me with warm, loving eyes.

She said: 'Have you got Lyme disease? I'm so sorry for you!' I will never forget this. Since that time, I know exactly whether people react from their hearts or from their minds. Unfortunately, it has been statistically proved that 25% of the friends of people diagnosed with a serious, life-threatening disease break their friendship. This is very painful since one needs the support of friends to recover from a disease that has such an impact.

However, it is very important to stay optimistic and keep on believing in miracles when you are seriously ill. When I was in a very poor and severe condition, I visualised being connected with the healing primal power of the earth via strong roots coming from my feet. Then I visualised a dome of white healing light around me, coming from the Divine Dimension.

In my life, magical things happen, like the wagtail bird couple tapping on the window in Holland, in the middle of winter, while I was in the restroom. In the afternoon, that same bird couple tapped on the window on the other side of the house when I was about to have a shower. These little miracles gave me hope in my darkest lyme disease period.

But this is nothing compared with the big miracle that happened shortly afterwards:

It was February and I was longing to return to Tuscany but I was too weak to travel.

I decided to invite the Universe to help me. I made a copy of the map of Italy and glued a photo of me standing in front of a coffee bar, feeling very happy, on the Tuscany province. Every time I went to the toilet, I longingly looked at the photo and guess what happened… A man, who used to be my lover a long, long time ago, contacted me. He was living and working in Australia and felt an irresistible need to contact me. I was so excited to see him again and I booked a romantic hotel suite. I felt insecure since I was using crutches and looked like a wounded little bird. However, I was very attracted to him and my heart said YES, very loudly and clearly!!! The rest is history; within no time we left for Tuscany and he really looked after me, which enabled me to recover from the symptoms of Lyme disease. To me, this is the perfect example of the power of creative visualization. I tell you more about this power in the chapter: 'The beneficial effect of mindfulness'.

GENUINE COMMUNICATION

It is so simple, and yet we often make it unnecessarily complicated. When you are hungry, then you should eat; when you are thirsty, then you should drink; and when you have a feeling, then you should express that feeling in the first person. If you express your feeling you will maintain a sense of connectedness to that person, but if you hold it back then you will be blocked off and the friendship or relationship will stagnate.

It is of great importance that from now on you try only to be yourself, with all your positive, but also what you perceive to be your negative sides and show it to the outside world.

BE HONEST REGARDING YOURSELF AND OTHERS

Many people think one thing, say another thing and do yet another. It costs a mountain of energy when day in, day out you project yourself in a way that is not true to how you actually are. For as long as you keep certain parts of yourself hidden away from others, you must remain constantly on your guard that you are acting "as if". You have to be ever watchful that no-one discovers the 'real you', and you have no proper idea what to do with yourself. In this way you lose your natural vivacity and spontaneity, and thereby also your natural power of attraction.

Be honest and sincere about yourself and your fellow people. Being just who you really are, at this moment in time, with both your lighter and your darker sides, is infinitely better than keeping your darker sides hidden.

To achieve this we must first cast away an established norm that has been spoon-fed to us since infancy, namely that it is a sign of weakness to present yourself as being vulnerable. (Boys in particular have had to swallow far too much of this slop!)

As I have previously stated:

The opposite is true. Allowing yourself to be seen as vulnerable is actually a sign of strength, because this requires courage.

You will notice time and again that when you dare to show your vulnerability, those around you will feel able to do the same, and only then can genuine contact between you exist. If you find it awkward to present your 'naked' self in this way, then you can try it out first in a situation that feels safe for you. Of course there will always be people who feel so inferior and frustrated that they are constantly seizing on the so-called weaknesses of others who come across as being vulnerable. Whenever I encounter this attitude, I immediately say that I do not appreciate it and do not wish to be treated in this way. If the person in question does not take up on this then I break off contact with them, because I would rather not be dealing with such a person.

And in due course, other people who do attach value to genuine communication will soon be crossing my path. Before I became more enlightened about it, I used to be afraid to let others see those aspects of my personality of which I did not approve myself. I was alarmed by such notions as: "If they see that side of my nature, they will surely disapprove and break off our friendship". In actual fact, the opposite turned out to be true - no disapproval would follow, at most a little positive criticism here and there.

My friendships have actually intensified and been enriched as a result, and I am now more able to appreciate others' points of view.

I realise with hindsight however that at times I could be *too* open, honest or expansive. It is not necessary to bare your soul wide open for everyone to see. Every person has the right to carry within themselves a 'sealed jar' with the tenderest and most vulnerable contents, and may themselves decide when they think the time is right to remove the seal and allow someone else to take a look inside.

YOU CAN LEARN HOW TO COMMUNICATE

I now present to you a few rules of thumb for productive communication:

1. Express yourself in the right way

I always say: "Express yourself, otherwise you'll give yourself a stomach ache; but be sure to express yourself in the right way, or else you'll end up giving someone else a stomach ulcer."

2. Always speak in the first person

State as clearly and specifically as possible what you are wanting to say. Don't say for example "You're such a rotter", but rather "You're being so rotten to me", or better still "What you're doing really upsets me and makes me feel rotten." Many people make this mistake and many parents indulge endlessly in such behavior towards their children. They do not realise that by doing so they are seriously undermining their children's developing senses of self-value.

3. **Be assertive**

Stand up assuredly and resolutely for yourself and your own interests - but without thereby harming the interests of others. Confront people when you feel you are being treated unjustly. You will achieve the most when you demonstrate strength and when you persist with your point for as long as it takes to be listened to.

4. **Ask first for clarification in cases of misunderstanding**

Suppose for example that a good friend informs you that someone has been bad-mouthing you. Do not furiously confront that person with an immediate counter attack, but ask first if what you have been told is indeed true.

5. **What you say often comes across very differently to how you intended it**

Many people have a tendency not to listen very well, and frequently when they recount your story it is from their own personal viewpoint.

The true reality of the situation up getting lost, only to be replaced by different interpretations of that reality.

Erase "I know I'm right" from your vocabulary. If you find you cannot agree on something, then say "I see that we are not able to agree on this point so I propose we let it rest for the time being, and broach another subject". In this way everyone is left with their own assessment of the situation intact. Problems with communication also frequently arise between men and women, the roots of which lie in classical conditioning. Men in general react in a rational way, whereas women on the other hand - despite their two-sided development - tend to rely more on their intuition. John Gray has written two interesting books that shed new light on this subject: *Men are from Mars, Women are from Venus* and *Men, Women and Relationships*.

6. Accept that life is a mass of contradictions

Contrasting ideas are able to exist side by side until a new unity arises. View all conflicts between yourself and others as an essential part of your growth process.

One very well-known conflict, for example, is that between the need for security and the need for freedom. Until you have discovered your True Self, you are still made up of several sub-persons each with their own particular needs, which regularly find themselves at loggerheads with each other. This can explain why people so often fail to fulfil their promises.

One sub-person promises one thing, but then another sub-person that sees no chance of honouring the promise takes over.

7. Be aware of the phenomenon of projection

This is one of the most elusive problems in human communication. Projection comes into play when someone prefers not to recognise an unattractive aspect of their own self, and instead "projects" that aspect onto someone else before proceeding to attack it. In this way someone who has difficulty in remaining honest can accuse a friend, who may always be completely honest, of dishonesty. This can drive the accused to despair and is disastrous for an intimate relationship, because both partners are so fused together.

It is also very important to bear this in mind whenever someone is being critical of you. There is a saying, that when we criticise someone we are pointing with two fingers (thumb and index finger) at them and the other three at ourselves. Psychology calls the projection phenomenon a **defence mechanism**, in which the ego resists dangerous, inadmissible or painful impulses that are trying to break through into one's consciousness.

THE BENEFICIAL EFFECT OF MINDFULNESS

MASTER YOUR MIND! REVEAL YOUR SUB-PERSONALITIES

Until the moment we truly know ourselves, we find ourselves in the unpleasant position of being a passenger in our own car of life (or worse, being trapped in the trunk) while our sub-personalities are taking turns driving it.

Hal Stone and Sidra Winkelman wrote a very valuable book together: *Embracing Ourselves*. They very clearly describe the situation most of us are in, within in the current society.

THE DEVELOPMENT OF OUR SUB-PERSONALITIES

Each and every baby comes into this world with its own genetic make-up and a special, unique essence. Stone & Winkelman call this the essence level of the newborn.

I would rather call it the level of the True Self. No other creature is as defenseless as a newborn baby, totally dependent on its parents for food and nurturing love.

The child soon finds out that he/she needs to make a significant effort to get what he/she needs. Whenever the baby smiles, the mother smiles. A smelly nappy makes her pull a face. And this continues for the next 21 years; certain behavior is being rewarded, other behavior is being punished. In other words, certain parts of us will be reinforced, others will be weakened.

This can be achieved in very subtle ways by for instance raising an eyebrow, or in very cruel ways, including heavy punishments and humiliations. We gradually loose contact with our True Self during this process and we start developing all kinds of sub-personalities in order to survive in our complex, industrialized society.

We are no longer the creators of our lives. Instead we have become 'pawns on a chessboard', servants of market laws and profit seeking, and get trapped in possessiveness and greed. We have forgotten who we really are and what we really want. Our minds rule and we are no longer connected to our hearts.

THE HEAVYWEIGHTS

Heavyweights are sub-personalities (energy patterns) that are gradually forced into our systems as we are being raised. The most familiar heavyweights are:

1. The pusher

2. The critic

3. The perfectionist

4. The pleaser

   1. The **pusher** is the sub-personality that is always chasing us with a whip in one hand and an unfinished to-do list in

the other. This to-do list never ends; the grass needs mowing, the tap is dripping, you need to finish your thesis etcetera. It doesn't allow us to rest and relax. Our **pusher** can be a true devil, able to completely destroy us with its extreme demands. This makes people with a dominant PUSHER more likely to have a heart attack.

2. The **critic** continuously wants us to feel bad about ourselves. It effortlessly and cold-heartedly knows how to hit our weakest spots.
3. The **perfectionist** wants us to do everything perfectly right. It doesn't accept any C grades; they all have to be straight A's!

The pusher, critic and perfectionist make up a dangerous trio together, capable of taking us on the verge of a total collapse.

1. The **pleaser** consists of a totally different energy pattern. Especially women risk to be ruled by this sub-personality. The kind of women that ignore themselves, are always available and are having trouble setting boundaries. With their eternal smile on their face they will ignore themselves wherever they can in order to be able to offer a helping hand.

While studying Psychosynthesis, I discovered a very dominant **pleaser** inside of me and I called this sub-personality 'the mother hen'. The mother-hen in me was very sensitive to the needs of all people, animals and even plants in her area. Whenever someone was in need of help, she couldn't resist offering a helping hand without setting any boundaries to protect her own needs. She would never wonder whether she actually had the time and energy to offer all the help people were asking for (or weren't asking for) and whether her help was actually useful. Nothing was too much for me. In the seventies, my doors were open to give shelter to a runaway youngster and to a Norwegian feminist woman. This woman once asked me my permission to bring over some fellow Norwegian ladies in order to discuss the higher feminist ideals. I was a 'Dolle Mina' (which means: 'Mad Mina', a social-feminist activist group) myself at the time, so in my eyes I couldn't refuse. However, I forgot to ask how many 'sisters' were involved in this sleep-over. I came home late that night and to my dismay I tripped over the large number of Norwegian feminists in sleeping bags. The whole house, including the hallway and the living-room, was covered with them. I couldn't even reach my kitchen. But what was I to do? All these feminist women were fast asleep; waking them up now was not an option. So, I ended up pussyfooting to my bedroom, carefully avoiding to step on the sleeping bags and their content (gratefully using my experience I gained during the Kralingen pop festival in Rotterdam).

During the eighties, I was having a hard time coping with several jobs at the same time, when, in addition, I decided to give shelter to a confused female student writing her essay. She stayed for several weeks and continuously asked for my attention.

In my rare spare time, I helped her writing her essay and was her therapist at the same time.

Today the above mentioned two examples from a long list of similar situations make me laugh. However, they also made me end up being prematurely burnt-out.

It took me years to realize I was always looking after and helping everyone but myself and to see that this was very self-destructive behaviour.

Somewhere around my fortieth birthday, I was completely exhausted which forced me to take a good look in the mirror and to command my mother hen to take a step back. I completely ran out of energy to help others.

I had ended up in a danger-zone and, due to (amongst others) a Hypoglycemic Syndrome, turned into a zombie. I had to learn to surround myself with an abundance of love and attention and to set and strictly monitor my own boundaries.

The Universe first gently taps us on the shoulders to make something clear. If we don't pay attention, it will start hitting us harder and harder. Some people just have to bang with their heads against the wall before they become aware of the message.

A woman who has allowed the pleasing energy pattern dominating her life should wisely cultivate a healthy level of selfishness.

REVEALING YOUR SUB-PERSONALITIES

Now I will teach you how to detach from your sub-personalities and to get back in the driver's seat of your own car of life permanently.

First, we need to understand that the energy patterns of our sub-personalities are not necessarily good or bad by nature. They can have both positive and negative qualities. Stone & Winkelman explain it like this:

The key is not to be ruled by the negative qualities but to consciously decide to make the positive qualities work for us.

Without the **pusher** pushing me, I would have never been able to write my books. However, I learned to control it and no longer allowed it to make me work too hard and too fast. I did not want to write with a deadline pressure; I wanted my writing to be encouraged by inspiration, creativity and joy. And I succeeded!

The **critic** and the **perfectionist** also needed to be controlled. Realizing that life is all about learning, makes it easier to succeed.

The **critic**, however, also has positive qualities we can benefit from. It will point out what is going wrong and what needs our attention.

And the qualities of the **perfectionist** help us with all the detailed work in this world that needs a great extent of accuracy.

There is only one way to liberate yourself from identification with your sub-personalities: the way to awareness. The key is to step out of the world of your sub-personalities and observe them and their behaviour from a distance.

As soon as you start working with your sub-personalities, a fascinating process begins. And your efforts will be increasingly rewarded.

You will discover that each step out of the world of your sub-personalities is a step into the world of your True Self. In other words; the more you liberate yourself from the identification with your sub-personalities, the more you will experience your True Self.

The snowball effect will do its work; the further you get in the awareness process, the faster the snowball will roll since the positive effects will increasingly reinforce each other. Based on my own experience, I can assure you how incredibly good it feels to come home to your True Self. It provides you with a sense of faith in your destiny, inner peace, joy, gratitude and it makes you feel connected to your fellow human beings, animals and nature. Your True Self grants you a still point in the midst of all the noise you are surrounded by. What's more, it gives you the feeling you are the creator of your own life; you drive your own car of life towards the destinations you have chosen yourself. Your sub-personalities are your passengers and will carry out the commands you give them in order to reach those destinations.

This teamwork will result in an excellent harmony where your True Self will always perfectly indicate which energy pattern is needed for any particular situation.

To everyone who wants to reveal their sub-personalities, I strongly recommend to check out the book *Embracing Ourselves* by Hal Stone and Sidra Winkelman.

Another option is to look for someone who specializes in the 'Voice Dialogue' method or Psycho synthesis. While working with your dominant sub-personalities, do not forget to bring in your sense of humor. No matter how dramatic things seem to be, laugh at yourself while having no control at all being a passenger at the back seat of your car of life, or worse, lying in the trunk. And decide not to live like this any longer!

As long as we live an unconscious life, we all make mistakes. The only thing we can do is to forgive ourselves and each other for our mistakes and be highly committed to our awareness process.

WHO AM I? AND WHAT DO I REALLY WANT!

We do in our lives many things automatically without asking ourselves if we really want to do them. As long as you do not know if you really want something, things happen to you, outside yourself. If you undergo your fate passively life is often like a steamroller that threatens to crush you. You are out of control and your sub-personalities are busy all day to respond to your surroundings.

Suppose you are working on something important and the bell rings. The one on the doorsteps asks: 'Am I intruding?' But 'the kind in you' says, 'No, come in, do you want some coffee?' Why don't we dare to say: 'Actually I have no time, so let's make an appointment for another time ".

I give you now an exercise that I have used for years in my training to women:

Grab a pen and paper and make a list of everything you must, or you are obliged to do from yourself, others or the society.

For example:

I have to earn € 2,000 net each month. I must be a good mother or father.

I have to clean my house every day. Every Sunday I have to visit my parents. And so on.

Please listen while you are making this list to the signals of your body? How does it feel?

Draw a big cloud and write in it everything you really want:

For example:

I want to become a good pianist.

I want to spend the winter in a warm country. I want to help children in the third world.

I want to have a loving partner and so on.

And again note what is happening in your body?

Now compare the body signals of the first list with everything you MUST do with the second list with everything you really WANT TO DO.

Do you notice the difference?

Generally spoken there is a body-protest when you must do all kind of things, you don't really like to do in the form of short of breath and tense. On the other hand the body will be open and relaxed when you do things that you really like.

Finally, there is this exercise for you in order to establish a deeper connection to your True Self.

Do I fully coincide with my body?

No, I HAVE my body, I AM not my body Do I fully coincide with my thoughts?

No, I HAVE my thoughts, I AM not my thoughts Do I fully coincide with my depression?

No, I HAVE a depression, I AM not my depression

MY THOUGHTS WILL ARISE AND THEN DISAPPEAR, MY TRUE SELF HOWEVER WILL ALWAYS BE HERE

Who is this person, this 'I' behind all these thoughts? It is your True Self! We need to learn only to think when necessary and stop useless thinking and worrying since this makes us loose energy and build up tension. As soon as you stop thinking, you are able to experience your True Self being the center of infinite consciousness.

MEDITATION RESTORES THE CONTACT WITH OUR TRUE SELF

Meditation is a very powerful and effective way to get to know your True Self. The self that you were born with. It helps you to fully direct your attention inward. This deactivates your common thinking patterns and opens your

intuitive channel, allowing you to connect to your inner being.

In addition, meditation has a very positive impact on your body and mind. In his book *Meditation for Everybody* Louis Proto reveals the impressive effects of meditation on a regular basis. These effects have been confirmed by 350 different kinds of research. To everyone who is interested in more information on the beneficial effects of meditation I highly recommend this book to base your practice and further study on.

BELOW I WILL GIVE YOU A LIST OF A FEW OF THE EFFECTS:

1. Physical benefits: psychosomatic complaints, caused by psychic-mental tension, will disappear. The energy battery will be recharged and the immune system will be reinforced.
2. Psychic benefits: you will disassociate from your problems, will be provided with clarity and integrate (unite) all kinds of contradictions. Your self-consciousness will grow.
3. Rational benefits: you will be able to focus better, your memory will be improved, you will learn quicker and gain more creative ideas.
4. Benefits in the game of life: your senses are being increasingly stimulated, you will be more alert and take things less seriously which will increase your joy of life.
5. Relational benefits: your self-confidence will grow, you will become more authentic, more sensitive and more tolerant.

Last but not least, meditating on a regular basis will lead to a decrease of the need to use caffeine, tobacco, alcohol and drugs.

Regular meditation helps us to relax in a natural way and to achieve a better balance, which is so much better than taking in all those tranquillizers.

I'm pretty sure no other activity on earth leads to as many benefits as meditating does!

Why aren't there more tv programmes that teach us about the healing powers of meditation, or programmes that introduce us to the various ways of helping ourselves to become a consciously living and loving human being?

There are many meditation techniques, including meditations where the body is moving and meditations where the body is unmoving. You don't necessarily have to sit in a Lotus position. You are free to release your emotions in a dynamic Osho meditation or in the Latihan meditation by Bapak Subud. Another option is to go into nature, sit against a tree (or simply in your own house on a chair) and follow your breath. Most people breathe very superficially (chest breathing) while you take in so much more oxygen when you breathe deeply into your abdomen. Start by inhaling for a count of four and exhaling for a count of four. As soon as this feels okay, you can start breathing deeper. Meditation is about switching off your mind to get in touch with your deeper feelings in order to be able to receive important messages from your pure intuition. You could add a sound like 'sharim' or 'shadan', or another sound that resonates within you. Silently repeat that sound and whenever thoughts are coming up, just let them pass by and focus on your sound again. If you do this once a day for about fifteen minutes, you will already notice a positive change.

I practiced about seven meditation techniques but the Latihan technique impressed me the most. I used to participate in a women's meditation group in Amsterdam once every week. After a signal, every woman would tune into her 'deeper emotional impulses' and would receive messages from her higher consciousness at the same time. All women would move across the room with their eyes closed, singing, dancing, laughing, crying and stamping their feet with inner anger. However, nobody bumped into each other and the sounds all the women produced sounded like a harmony. That to me is magic. After the meditation we had tea together and I felt reborn. I received many messages from my intuition, which turned out to be crucial for my personal development. I learned that releasing your negative emotions results in a positive flow. Therefore, Latihan is not just a meditation but also a transformation and purification process. That is why several exploratory meetings are essential before someone can take part in the group sessions.

Meditation, mind control, positive thinking, sincere communication empathy and compassion should all be taught in schools.

Research has shown that we are causing damage to our immune system by producing negative mental patterns, such as bitter, long-lasting resentment and feelings of guilt. Negative thoughts create toxins or 'chemical messages' that find their way into our blood. These toxins not only poison our blood but our minds too. However, the greatest damage is caused by a negative self-image.

The best guarantee for good health and happiness is acceptance of, and unconditional love for, yourself. It's actually quite simple: self-knowledge is where wisdom starts. You can only truly love another human being if you truly love

yourself and you can only see the beauty in others if you are aware of your own beauty.

This also means that people who run down other people's accomplishments or humiliate them are merely projecting their own unfinished mental problems onto the other. Developing your awareness and healing your mental traumas is not only good for you but also for our social climate on earth.

CONSCIOUS LIVING IN THE HERE-AND-NOW

We must learn again to live in the here-and-now. That is to say that we are completely involved in the things we are doing and experience consciously the joy of all the beautiful things in our lives.

This is often very difficult for adults because most of us are still trapped in the past and bothered by painful experience. On top of that we are already bothered by being anxious about our future.

So we forget to experience consciously the present. In the industrial countries we are busy the whole time mentally and have little contact with our bodies. We need to open up and reawaken our senses and consciously see, hear, smell and taste.

We should specially remember our sixth sense: **intuitive feeling**. In this respect we can learn a lot from children: Look how they are fully absorbed in their game and enjoy every moment. Life is so short and our time is so precious. Let's enjoy it as much as we can! Many people are not able to live in a mindful way and to enjoy the blessings life has to offer. It is crucial to realize there are always two ways to experience reality. The choice is all up to you. If you've planned a visit to your dentist tomorrow, you can choose to feel really bad about it and have this visit spoil your whole day and evening. Or you could tell yourself what a blessing it is to live in a country where proper dental care exists. In the first case, you labeled the situation in a negative way, in the second case the positive label made you feel better. If you understand this principle, you are ready to work on a 'master-your-mind-plan'. First, you need to fully realize that you have your thoughts but you are not your thoughts. The following affirmation can be very helpful:

I have thoughts but I am not my thoughts. My thoughts come and go while I will always continue to exist. Therefore, from this moment on I choose to have positive thoughts in order to contribute to the quality of my life.

As soon as you understand this principle, you can start working with it. You can follow your own flow of thought and change this flow as soon as it starts to turn into a negative one. This is called 'positive affirmation'.

By saying STOP, you can interrupt the negative thought and turn it into a positive one. You will notice a positive change in your mental health which contributes to your wellbeing and to the wellbeing of the whole world at the same time.

Now look at the following sentences: 'Humanity is lost, all hope is gone', or 'I have faith in the fact that more and more people become aware of our global problems and that we are able to solve these problems by joining forces'. Can you feel the difference?

Finally, it is very important to forgive yourself for everything you have done wrong to yourself and other people. In general, people don't hurt each other consciously.

Mostly, they are not aware of the consequences of their actions.

A crucial aspect is the need for men to become mindful, since mindfulness is inextricably linked to being well-balanced. A state of balance can only be achieved if heart and mind are balanced.

Positive thinking has a positive impact on your health; it releases endorphins, the body's natural 'feel good' chemicals, which help to reinforce your immune system. It is important to realize that you always have a choice: you can focus on the things you have or focus on the things you don't have. In the first case you will be grateful for the abundance in your life and count your blessings. In the second case you will never be satisfied with the things you have and will always want more. You will be driven by greed and never find true happiness.

SPECIAL MESSAGE FOR (MULTI)MILLIONAIRES & BILLIONAIRES

There are (multi-)millionaires and billionaires who are giving decadent, extravagant dinners, where they treat their guests delicious food like a certain type of mussels (barnacles). This includes not only the taste but above the background story: it is told in 'scents and colours' that it is very difficult and dangerous to pick these mussels from the rocks in Galicia whereby five men in a year find a watery grave.

After their dinner they enjoy the taste of a cup of coffee that costs $300 due to the special flavour because the coffee beans were defecated by apes in Sumatra. The craziest is not crazy enough, and they are constantly in the search of new delights peppered with bizarre background stories.

I often wonder how it is possible that these superrich people enjoy their decadent lifestyle, while in the meantime hundreds of thousands innocent, sweet young children are dying from hunger and diseases.

Wake up and save these children because they are the most beautiful creatures in the world and they deserve a better fate. These children need your help!

Speaking of which, I have a special message for all those captains of industry who have gathered multi-(m)billions fortunes. Your (m)billions will only bring temporary pleasure but you will never find lasting happiness like the kind that results from saving innocent children who are ill or starving.

Realizing that your support can help to save a child, put a twinkle in its eyes and make it laugh again is guaranteed to give you feeling of deep and lasting happiness. It will touch your heart deeply and you will be reminded of the fact that you gave a child its life back everyday!

These children are victims of an unjust fate and are cruelly affected by the unequal distribution of food.

Follow the example of men like Bill Gates and Richard Branson and donate part of your capital to projects that fight poverty, famine and diseases. Leo Hindery jr. is a 'reluctant millionaire'. His media companies are worth 100 million dollar. However, he encourages the middle class to stand up and act against the fact the amount of tax they're paying is much higher than the tax paid by the richest people among us. He is a member of the 'patriotic millionaires', a group of millionaires you can only sign up for if you donate half of your capital to charity (see: www.patrioticmillionaires.org).

Follow the actions of, 'The secret millionaires' who leave their luxurious lives to go 'undercover' to discover the lives of the poor survivors. At the end they donate between 50.000 and 150.000 dollars. They all say this is a very positive life-changing experience.

RESTORE THE CONNECTION WITH NATURE

It is of great value to restore the connection with nature and realize that you are never alone. You are 'carried' by mother nature, hugged by the sun, refreshed by the wind and the rain and you are surrounded by beautiful flowers and around you the birds are singing their glamorous song.

These are blissful moments where you feel attached to a 'greater whole' and in these moments of bliss you can even experience ecstatic feelings. Just like a drop that gets lost from the ocean dries up, the human soul that does not feel anymore connected with a greater whole, will wither and perish.

I guarantee you: When you restore your contact with Mother Nature your soul will be nourished and your body will be healed from fatigue and stress. I always say: The sun and the sea are my best friends, because they never hurt me and bring me always warmth and refreshment. I have a lot of magical experience with butterflies.

When I am in my garden they often 'land on my body' and stay a while with me. Once I opened my door and I saw a huge butterfly (Vanessa Atlanta) and a toad sitting together at my doormat, looking in my direction.

I said hello what are you doing here? What is the meaning of your visit?

These are fascinating, inspiring moments that make me realize there is more between heaven and earth than we can imagine…

HOW TO ACHIEVE WHAT YOU REALLY WANT

Follow the master-your-mind action plan below:

1. **Fully focus on your target. Take action and support this process with creative visualization.**
2. **Stand up for yourself and establish and maintain clear boundaries.**
3. **Targeted action and creative visualisation.**

Make your dreams come true today. Don't wait until you are 65 because it might be too late. If you want to make your dreams come true it is very important to base your focus on two pillars.

The first pillar is called **targeted action**. Which means you systematically take practical steps on a daily basis while being fully focused and determined. If, for instance, you dream of a house by the sea, visit as many real estate agents as you can and try to excite them for your dream house with your enthusiasm. In addition, you can place adverts in the local papers and search online.

The second pillar is called **creative visualization**. Which means you very clearly and vividly visualize you target, using all your senses. Let's say you want to exchange a life in the city for the tranquility of the countryside. Clearly and vividly picture your new house and home town. Cut out pictures and create a collage of the kind of house that you dream of. Draw or paint your perfect house or combine these techniques; cut out a picture of your dream house and paint a whole forest around it. Use lots of colours and don't forget to add **yourself** to the picture; cut out a photo and put yourself in the doorway as the proud owner. You can add written words to it: 'I really enjoy my new house and garden'. Look at this collage more than once every day! Is it a house by the sea, then smell the fresh sea air and feel the wind caressing your hair. Actively work with this image several times a day, specially right after waking up and just before going to sleep.

Be truly convinced you deserve live in this house. That you're worth it and will end up getting it. Block every negative thought and every doubt. Let them drift away like clouds in the sky and convince yourself over and over again the house of your dreams will come your way.

BASIC PRINCIPLES OF CREATIVE VISUALISATION

Creative visualization will be most beneficial if you truly understand the basic principles it is based on. I will discuss them using my own experience and the book *Creative Visualization* by Shakti Gawain. In natural sciences, the proof that we all (and everything in and around us) consist of energy is becoming increasingly evident. We are all connected to one huge energy field. (Which, by the way, our spiritual teachers have been aware of for centuries.) Our thoughts are a fast, light, flexible form of energy that, contrary to more dense forms (like physical matter), manifests quickly.

To us, it is normal to have an architect make a design and have a contractor build the house based on this design. We have to get used to the fact that our thoughts create a blueprint that tends to become reality. If you always think you will become ill, you significantly increase the risk of actually becoming ill. Everyone will understand that a farmer using bad seed on a rocky soil will end up with a poor harvest.

The idea of creating poor living conditions by producing negative thoughts however, seems strange to us. Yet, the bible makes a clear statement in this regard: 'sow the wind, reap the whirlwind'.

This means that we will always attract what we think of most, what we strongly believe in, what we clearly imagine and what we are really convinced of deep inside. Be aware that active creative visualization doesn't involve (superficial) positive thinking.

It involves tracing and deeply investigating your fundamental approach to life.

During this process, we discover that we are interfering with our own happiness by blocking ourselves with our fears and negative way of thinking. In other words, we unconsciously sabotage our own happiness.

I clearly remember being introduced to this principle, thinking: 'Okay, I will fix this in no time'. I was having financial problems at the time and quickly did my visualization ritual while walking the dogs. I pictured piles of banknotes flying towards me. Unfortunately, the situation didn't change. Later, I understood that, on a much deeper level, an old negative message was still actively resonating: 'You don't deserve for all this to become reality.' It encouraged me to learn more about the **no-current** and the **yes-current** by Eva Pierrakos. On a superficial level it seems as if you really want something but on a deeper level a negative self-image tells you 'No, you don't deserve it!' You need to work on this first.

For an effective way of creative visualization, Shakti Gawain provides us with the action plan below:

1. Determine your goal

Select a goal that means a lot to you, is easy to believe in and reachable within the near future. (Later, when you are more experienced, you can focus on higher goals that you think may take more time to reach.

2. Create a clear image

Always think in the present tense; as if the situation you wish for has already become reality. Make the image as detailed as possible.

3. Frequently tune in on your goal

Visualize the image you created of your goal as frequently as you can during the day, especially immediately after waking up and just before you go to sleep. In addition, visualize it during your meditation.

4. Give it positive energy

Always talk to yourself in a positive way. Say it is possible, that now you will really make it happen. Picture yourself receiving or achieving it.

These positive messages are called **affirmations or confirmations**. If you are planning to use them, keep the following facts in mind:

1. Always express an affirmation in the present tense. Say, for instance, 'I have a wonderful new job', instead of 'I will get a wonderful new job', since this is a future expectation.
2. Always confirm what you **want**, not what you **don't want**. So don't say 'I won't oversleep anymore'. Instead use 'from now on I will get up on time and full of energy every morning
3. Use simple, short and powerful affirmations since they work best.
4. Always choose affirmations that you think are entirely right and suitable.
5. Try your utmost to really believe your affirmations.

Temporarily (at least for a few minutes) let go of all
negative thoughts, doubts and resistance.

6. Don't gabble your affirmations but make the feeling you
truly have the power to create your own reality grow ever
stronger.

7. Affirmations are even more powerful and inspiring if
they refer to spiritual sources, for instance: 'The divine
love is flowing through me, here and now, to create this.'
If you feel resistance using the word 'divine', you could
say, 'I am one with my higher self and I have an infinite
creative power.'

Expressing positive affirmations may bring up resistance in you
since we were all brought up with negative messages. The ego
will fight any change tooth and nail. You need to make an effort to
make the ego stop fighting.

GO WITH THE FLOW

Shakti Gawain refers to an ancient principle of Taoism called 'Go
with the flow' which is vital to effective creative visualizations.
Going with the flow means that getting where you want to be does
not require big efforts. Clearly and vividly send your goal (wish
or dream) into the Universe and patiently follow your life path
until it takes you there.

Your life path will not always lead straight to your goal.
Sometimes it meanders towards it or it will even lead you to a
temporary opposite direction.

**Go with the flow means lightly holding on to your goals
without clinging to them since this will have the opposite
effect.**

It also means you have to be willing to adjust and redirect your goals in case something happens along the way that grants you more fulfilment. In other words, you need to be both persisting as well as flexible.

You could compare this with planting seeds. You pick a sunny, appropriate spot, remove the stones and weed and plant the seeds into the soil. You water them in dry periods and wait patiently, while regularly thinking of the future magnificent beauty of blooms and blossoms you will be able to witness. However, if you are impatient and dig up the seeds every day to check whether they are sprouting, you will disrupt the growing process. In case you are too emotionally involved ('I really, really, really need that house, girl-/boyfriend etc.'), it may be useful to verify what is you fear if you will not get it. Then first use affirmations in order to increase your self-confidence and feeling of security in order to overcome your fear.

I would like to stick to the Taoist principle 'Go with the Flow' a little longer. Obviously, simply leaning back and wait until your dreams come flying towards you after having sent the message into the Universe doesn't work. In addition to creative visualization, you also need to take the necessary practical steps to reach your goal.

REALIZATION OF MY DREAMHOUSE IN TUSCANY

I will give you a nice example of the effortless way an old dream of mine - a house in Tuscany! - came true. When my three jobs still forced me to rush around all day, I dreamt of living in a house in Tuscany together with an abundance of peace and freedom allowing me to draw and paint.

I had been in Florence once and this city, being the cradle of the Renaissance, and the Tuscan scenery had struck me so deeply that my dream stayed with me. Seven years later, I decided it was time to make my dream come true and put the crazy idea to drive to Tuscany with a friend, armed with two tents and the words 'Voglio una casa' ('I want a house'), into practice.

We arrived at the overcrowded campsites at the hottest time of the day, welcomed by incredibly loud transistor radio music; for the Italians it was holiday time. My first thought was 'over my dead body! I'd rather sleep in a ditch!' I suggested to drive along a minor road and ask permission to camp on a farmer's land. I was so happy when the first farmer we talked to allowed us to set up our tent somewhere in his olive grove. I was over the moon and every morning I enjoyed a cold shower by the garden house among the Tuscan chickens. Soon, the farm owners, Roberto and Maria, invited us over for dinner. When they found out we were looking for a house to rent, they told us they had another house that was only used for the wine grape harvest. The next day, they took us to 'Podere Santa Silvia', a simple house with a plain Tuscany interior but we felt like royalty. They offered us to rent the place for 300 Dutch Guilders and even allowed us to rent it out to other people.

After thoroughly renovating the place and adjusting it to our personal taste, our friends and us truly enjoyed this amazing opportunity that was given to us just like that.

It is very important to realise the Universe is an infinite horn of plenty giving us whatever we wish for, both materially as well as spiritually.

Most of us are having a hard time to really comprehend this idea of **prosperity programming** since we were raised with a **poverty programming**, learning things like: 'Life is tough and complicated, full of suffering and sorrow; You need to work hard and sacrifice for everything you receive' etcetera.

These concepts are wrong, based on a limited and wrong insight in the way the Universe works. Shakti Gawain states the following:

Currently, famine and poverty is reality for many people in this world but we don't have to keep on creating this reality and make it continue. It's a fact that there is more than enough to allow each and every creature on this earth to make a proper living, if only we are willing to open our minds for the possibility.

Shakti Gawain. *Creative Visualization.*

THE IMPORTANCE OF HEART - MIND - CONNECTION

The word mindfulness is actually - if you take it literally - an incomplete word. A person is in harmony and well balanced when he/she is both mindful and heartful. I see everywhere in the world a lack of heartfulness as a result of the increasing commercialization. It's so easy to say *'I love you'*, but if these words are not carried by loving behavior it brings people into confusion. When you truly love a person you give the other the space to be him/herself without all kinds of judgments and help the other to find his/her True Self and true passion and destiny. Judging is only useful if people damage themselves (or others) by destructive behavior.

REAL LOVE IS SUPPORTED BY EMPATHY AND COM-PASSION

If anyone should apply the golden rule, written in the bible: 'do unto others as you would have them do unto you' the world would be a paradise.

So all you have to do is working with great dedication on the increase of your consciousness. Be aware of who you are and what you doing. Ask yourself if your behavior contributes to the wellbeing of yourself, your fellowmen and the world. This concerns specially all men that have an underdeveloped emotional life and are unable to realize a heart – mind – connection. Be inspired by the wise words of the Dalai Lama in his wake-up-call: 'Never Give Up'.

Never Give Up
No matter what is going on
Never give up

Develop the heart
Too much energy in your country
is spent in developing the mind
instead of the heart
Develop the heart
Be compassionate
not just to your friends
but to everyone
Be compassionate
Work for peace
in your heart and in the world
Work for peace
and I say again
Never give up
No matter what is happening
No matter what is going on around you
Never give up!

The Dalai Lama

According to our original spiritual nature we are connected to the Divine energy (If you don't believe in God, you can also call it the Universal energy) and we are united with our fellow men and nature. And it is precisely this unity that gives us a sense of happiness fulfilment and security. The greatest danger of our outward conditioning is that we lost this natural state of connectedness. We live in the illusion that we are separated from our fellow men and we lose our energy in competition instead of working together in cooperation.

It is essential that we restore this connection and consider the others like our fellow creatures, who just like us are struggling with traumatic experience out of the past and a negative self image. In this sense we are all the same: we are in search of happiness and we are all avoiding pain and sorrow.

MEN AND WOMEN HAVE THE RIGHT TO MEANINGFUL WORK

When I look at all the work that is done on a daily basis in factories and offices around the world, my conclusion is that the majority of this work consists of dull, routine activities. I can hardly imagine that people actually enjoy doing this for 45 years without being offered any variation or challenges.

People have the natural urge to create something from the starting point, in order for them to be proud of a final result that reflects their True Self. It's human nature. A farmer who experiences the whole process of sowing through to harvesting gives meaning to his life, as is also the case for, say, a sculptor creating his own works of art. Creative work like this contains intrinsic ('self-rewarding') value.

Most routine factory or office work, on the other hand, has an extrinsic value; people work on just a part of the larger (invisible) whole and are rewarded at the end of the month by receiving their wages. These wages allow them to do desirable and necessary things.

In this sense, our current labour system is an affront to our natural creative qualities and our natural design. (The creativity of our children proves my statement!)

Very few people realise that our current separation between home and work has been foisted upon us since the year 1760, at the start of the industrial revolution in England.

In his book *Arbeid, een eigenaardig medicijn* (which means: Labour, a peculiar drug), Hans Achterhuis explains how men and women, before the industrial revolution, worked together in small-scale agricultural or artisan enterprises in order to meet their basic needs. The hard, multifaceted work of women was so much more appreciated and respected than the unpaid 'housewife job' of today.

This huge and drastic change was realised by violently chasing the farmers off their property and taking their land away from them. If the farmers showed any resistance, torture and branding methods were used to compel these people to comply to the new form of employment. In Amsterdam, disobedient people were forced into a 'water room' that was gradually filled with water. Some people preferred being drowned to being forced to work in factories.

In the beginning men, women and children were all forced into the factories together to carry out their 'forced labour' for poverty wages in barbaric circumstances.

The more vocal, 'bold and brassy' employees were subsequently compelled to remain silent by dealing separately with men on the one hand, and women and children on the other.

Women and children were banished to their homes, where the women were forced to carry out unpaid housework and to look after and raise their children, while their husbands exhausted themselves working ridiculously long hours in order to make a living for their wives and children.

In this way the powers that be managed to turn a rebellious mass of people into a disciplined labour force, says Achterhuis.

Today we are still dealing with the consequences of the industrial revolution, based on a separation between female and male types of employment and the exploitation of both sexes, where men are financially rewarded and women are expected to carry out 'loving and caring work' for free. Our current labour system including the work ethic 'Labour Ennobles' is an indirect result of this era.

The classic conditioning model, which has been taught endlessly via the various education methods of the time, is a result of this industrial production method, based on a separation of the sexes.

Men were always supposed to be raised as 'rational people' and women were reduced to merely 'emotional people'. These two types of 'half-developed' people were constantly dependent on each other. Men would receive their reward directly out of the state coffers, while women receive their 'salary' indirectly by being paid from their husbands' wages. Under the unfortunate (but frequent) circumstances of their husbands being alcoholics or gamblers who spent all their money, they would be eating stale bread. How remarkable it is, that the role of the man being the breadwinner (whether as a judge, a coal carrier or, like today, merely as a part of the monotonous production process, in factories or offices) was valued much more highly than the caring role of the woman!

After this thorough historical analysis, the only conclusion to be made is that this labour system was deeply flawed; it was

unnatural, it violated human dignity and it reduced women to second class citizens.

We currently live in a fascinating, though confusing, transition time. The classic conditioning system is rooted deeply within our bodies whereas the modern conditioning system is rooted inside our heads.

Do not underestimate the power of stereotypes!

Meanwhile, a lot has changed since the first and second feminist waves. Many women protested against their limited role, they caught up on their rational disadvantage and started participating in professional life and society as a whole. This has not been easy. In 1871 in Holland, Aletta Jacobs still had to fight to be the first woman to be admitted to the 'HBS' (college providing higher professional education, subsequently replaced by other types of college), and to university afterwards. Later, when she managed to become the first female doctor, many male doctors tried to impede her further progress. In other countries women also had to remove similar obstacles, for instance Maria Montessori in Italy.

Today, women are highly rationally **and** emotionally developed, which provides them with a great advantage over men, who in general just cling to their rational development. However, this advantage also involves a major risk. As long as the situation remains the same, women are being increasingly overburdened since they also have jobs outside their homes, while their husbands are not willing or unable, because of their over-stressful full time jobs, to contribute to housework sufficiently. In addition, women who are planning to build a career for themselves need to meet tough male criteria, which results in an even tougher society.

I do want to encourage men to pay attention to a proper caring and emotional development. I advocate a system where

men and women are both able to work part time, allowing them to also raise their children and carry out housework together, with duties shared equally.

Men have never, en masse, protested against their limited, rational development, which is odd. There are two reasons I can think of for this: men have been cut off from their emotions to such an extent they don't even realise that, deep in their hearts, they are not happy with their mainly boring jobs; and/or they have taken their role as pillars of economic progress so seriously that they actually believe their work is more important than raising children and doing housework.

As long as men only live a rational life, they are letting themselves down! They continually feel the need to be tough and heroic, to be responsible for the financial situation of their family, to hide their fear and insecurity and to force themselves to perform better every day. This is simply inhuman! No wonder men live an average of five years less than women do.

What's more, it is tragic how all these rational men completely lose contact with their pure intuition, and no longer feel that our current materialistic way of life damages humanity and our environment.

'The higher the career flies, the more hidden the heart lies'. Just watch your average top industrialist speaking on TV. You will see a robot talking, completely trapped in his own head. His face looks frozen and only his lips are moving. However, there is another major risk: purely rational men are far more easily involved in criminal violence than women, and they are sent to the frontline time and again, ending up as cannon fodder only because some world leaders feel the need to make war.

People with an open, empathic heart are not capable of harming other human beings in a violent way.

In fact, there have been men who were not willing to accept their limited role. They have organised protests and set up support groups for men to increase their awareness. Other men started working part-time in order to play a more active part in their family life. Often, they were sabotaged by their superiors. Some of these men started idealising their family caretaking activities and expected to be appreciated for it by the opposite sex. To their disappointment, however, they were often called 'softies' by women.

Certain women can be characterised by old, masochistic traits which make them feel attracted to the dominant kind of macho-man. Fortunately, more and more women have gained so much self-respect and self-esteem that they now prefer a both rationally *and* emotionally developed man, combining male strength with an emotional side, resulting in an essentially caring and nurturing character. But where to look for a man like this? Most men feel threatened by rationally and emotionally developed, powerful women. This results in the next problem: highly educated and socially successful women don't do too well on the marriage market. Which needn't be the case at all! If men were only able to get rid of their inner insecurity and confusion over which role to play, they would realise how much better it feels to be responsible for the family income together, instead of having to carry this heavy burden alone. And what bliss to be able to discuss all kinds of social issues with a partner who is not only rationally, but also emotionally well-developed!

Credit where credit is due! It's about time emotionally and rationally developed women receive the respect they deserve and the equal salary for their efforts to actively take part in

social life. To these women i would like to say: "Don't let your self-respect depend on men who have mostly become stuck in a limited, rational development. Respect yourself!"

Most men do not realise how precious it is to see their children grow up. Besides, it is a heavy and responsible job to guide children on their path to maturity in our current complex society. Men often don't know what they are missing out on in this era of absent fathers, while children really need to have their fathers present whilst growing up. Last, but certainly not least, our children can teach *us* so much. Babies and toddlers in particular are still very sensitive, spontaneous, honest and creative beings. They are never bored and completely lose themselves in the games they play. They are experts in mindfulness and they enjoy life to the fullest.

We, as adults, were forced to shed these qualities along the way. Most adults are trapped between their unfinished business of the past and their worries for the future, and are no longer capable of experiencing the joy of the moment.

Children help us to connect with our inner child, deeply buried underneath the armour of everything we were taught in order to survive in our current society.

Being connected to our children, we can learn how to empty our heads and to feel the needs of our hearts again. Together with our children we can dance, sing, draw or jump around, and free the power of our imaginations.

A PLEA FOR ORGANIC AGRICULTURE & CATTLE-BREEDING

Prior to the Industrial Revolution our ancestors lived in harmony with nature, and in terms of their food production they were self-sufficient. Their agriculture and livestock farming methods were small-scale and organic.

'MOTHER NATURE' ALWAYS KNOWS WHAT IS BEST FOR US

Nature can be regarded as being the wellspring of our health. If nature is allowed to take her course, then our own home environment can be seen to support a great variety of edible crops that contain the best micro-nutrients for maintaining a good health.

Scientific research has demonstrated that the so-called "hunter gatherer diet" provides the best ingredients for optimal health. This diet consists of edible plants and herbs, roots and tubers, nuts, seeds and wild fruits supplemented by meat and fish from wild animals.

It is remarkable that the crops that naturally grow around our homes are the very ones that keep us in the best of health, and it is evident that many primitive peoples who still sustain themselves in this way stay healthy for as long as they remain true to their original lifestyles.

This is also the way our own ancestors lived but now all the precious information on edible crops is at risk of being lost forever. People move to the cities in droves, although in times of crisis our chances of survival in the countryside are much better than they are in the city.

In our industrial world nature receives too little chance to grant us her benevolent bounty. Under asphalt roads and big cities, nature becomes suffocated.

The majority of our agriculture and horticulture has been taken into the hands of large-scale businesses and multinationals which use environmentally unfriendly methods such as artificial fertilizers and pesticides, resulting in vegetables and fruit which contain too few micro-nutrients to keep us in optimal health.

Furthermore, residues of pesticides are directly damaging to our health.

Small amounts of agricultural poisons in our food are already disrupting our hormone systems.

Do not let yourself be fooled by reports from the large-scale food industry that there is no difference between mainstream food from the supermarket and organic food. Only organic foods contain the micronutrients that keep us healthy!

SCANDALS AND ABUSE IN LARGE-SCALE LIVESTOCK FARMING

Around the year 2000 I wrote about the scandals and abuse in large-scale livestock farming. In addition to the incredible level of animal suffering resulting from cows and pigs not being able to graze and walk around in the fields and being forced into stables that are way too small, these poor animals are often transported for hours or even days in horrific circumstances to take them to the slaughterhouse. The Austrian Karreman used a hidden camera to film absolutely appalling scenes in which cows were forced onto the gangway of a ship in such a cruel way that the animals broke their legs. Afterwards, since the EU guidelines on correct livestock handling were unclear, one of the cows was forced back onto its legs using electric shocks, only to be subsequently chased off the ship. This resulted in its being thrown back onto the ship with the other animals with a big iron plate, after which it was facing further days of torture and abuse. Karreman was barely able to escape several assassination attempts following his documentary. Hopefully, many other people also saw the TV programme concerned and became just as sickened by it as I was. I won't force you to read the rest of the horrible details of the documentary.

However, I do want to draw your attention to an initiative of a certain Mr. Schweiger, who has advocated organic livestock breeding and the use of mobile abattoirs located in large trucks, meaning the animals do not have to suffer any longer during their horrific transportation. Besides this, the quality of the meat improves significantly; meat from animals that have suffered the cruelties such as those I mentioned during their last ordeals decreases enormously in quality. The stress, fear and panic of these animals results in a high level of glucose being stored in their bodies, and in addition muscles often start to bleed. All of this makes the meat tough and causes 'energetic pollution', meaning the suffering of the animals leaves a negative imprint in the meat. The Austrian documentary "The suffering of meat" was broadcast on Dutch television on 03-08-1999.

The very same year one of many other scandals was exposed, revealing the fact that there was currently no sufficient supervision of the administration of hormones to beef cattle. This resulted in the large-scale transportation of beef cattle from Belgium to the South of Holland in order to have the cows fed with forbidden hormone preparations. Within three months their weight went up from six to eight hundred kilos (The Dutch 'Volkskrant' newspaper, August 26 1999).

Karel van Noppen, the Belgian veterinarian who took action against the afore mentioned scandals, was killed.

Meanwhile, more and more scandals in the regular farming industries are being uncovered. All too often meat of unclear origin is put on the market, and horse meat is labelled as beef and sold in bulk. Hamburgers with no less than five kinds of processed meats have been discovered, making their origin too difficult to trace.

At the moment the lion's share of EU subsidies goes to intensive farming companies. Yet the demand for organic products keeps growing nonetheless.

This subsidy policy is wrong and should be re-evaluated, making less subsidy funds available for intensive farming and more for their organic alternatives instead.

Not only would this be better for our health, since organic food contains the most micronutrients, but also for the welfare of animals, for our environment and for food safety.

Industrial livestock production increases the risks of developing such diseases as swine flu, Creutzfeldt-Jakob disease (or BSE), Q fever, salmonella and Asian influenza (or bird flu). I believe that the health risks resulting from the consumption of meat coming from large-scale livestock production will only increase. For example hundreds of kilos of anthrax-infected meat were sold in The Netherlands.

The 'Netherlands Food and Consumer Product Safety Authority' was informed but kept silent on the matter.

In addition, the amount of milk being produced is no longer subject to quotas; the cow, treated as a milk factory, can be forced and manipulated into any condition the suppliers want them to be. Today, one third of all cows are forced to stay inside their stables throughout the whole year, while our country contains many vast green fields. And this will only become worse in the future. Seeing all those poor animals being locked up in stables that are way too small, with their heads down in their feed boxes, makes me incredibly sad.

In the Netherlands an incredible number of animals are crammed into mega-stables and when there is an outbreak of a disease, all the animals have to be killed.

On 18 December 2016, 38.000 chickens were killed because of the latest outbreak of bird-flu. Every day new slaughter takes place.

We, the consumers, should develop a critical consciousness: as long as we keep on buying meat and poultry from the large-scale, unnatural (and unsafe) supply chain, we are partly responsible for the suffering of animals and we are risking negative health consequences for ourselves.

Finally, reducing the amount of meat we consume also helps to cut global warming since the faeces of such a large number of farm animals produces large amounts of methane which contribute to global warming. Besides, eating less meat helps fight famine since all these animals eat huge amounts of corn that could be used to feed humans who are ill and dying of starvation.

THE DANGERS OF CURRENT LARGE-SCALE AGRICULTURE

We are poisoning our environment in such a way that an increasing number of bees are dying right now, and yet of course we need them for the pollination of our food.

These unique pollinators are an essential component in our food production.

There are strong indications that the biggest culprit among the insecticides is the group containing neonicotinoids. Seeds are being impregnated with these dangerous poison, which leads to poisoned plant saps and pollen.

Bees are weakened and disorientated by the poison, and can't find their way back to their hives. This dramatic news is affirmed by the German UBA (Umweltbundesamt). They want to ban 3 insecticides: imidacloprid, clothianidin, and thiametoxam and they recommend biological agriculture. This poison does not only affect the bees, but also other insects that visit the plants are affected.

In Holland and big parts of Germany, 75% of all insects disappeared already and this has a dramatic effect on the birds. The beautiful black cock died out already in Holland because there is not enough food for the little ones. One fourth of all insecticides contains these dangerous poison, and they also end up in the soil and surface water.

The British professor in biology Dave Goulson warns us that if we loose the insects the whole ecological system will collapse.

All the insecticides that contain neonicotinoids should be banned immediately to avoid a future food disaster.

Also the dubious Roundup of the producer "Monsanto" should be banned because it contains glyphosate. It destroys the biodiversity because it kills also the plants in surroundings. Moreover there are indications that Roundup causes cancer and disturbs our hormone system. There are alternative remedies like Raptol and Ultima of the producer "Ecostyle". *More info: www.ecostyle.nl*

It is inconceivable that the E.U. stil allows that Roundup available. That why it is so important to support "green" politicians like the Belgian Bart Staes who is fighting in the E.U. to ban Roundup.

Industrial agriculture is made up of many different multinationals that advocate large-scale monoculture, use of fertilizers, pesticides, and genetic modification techniques. In the book 'Demain la Terre' by Yannick Monget, about the effects of global warming, we read:

About the threat of pesticides:

"Fertilizers that farmers scatter frequently on their land are dangerous: only 10 percent of these substances are being absorbed by the plants. The remaining 90 percent is left in the environment, and turned into extremely toxic chemical compounds (nitric acid, nitrogen oxide and nitrate) that poison streams and surface water."

In addition, the vast single-crop fields used in large-scale industrial monocultures are increasingly exhausting our soils.

"Because of food industry lobbying we are forced to use and consume genetically modified organisms (GMO's), even when there is proof that these are harmful.Many tests on laboratory animals have clearly shown that the animals contract serious diseases as result of this."

The UN report on the right to food distinctly states: 'GMO's may be hazardous for the human organism and public health in the medium term or long run.' (Special UN-report on the right to food, November 2002).

At first the modification of living creatures' genetic material seemed to offer an amazing future: no more hunger, and even the least fertile land could be cultivated. Unfortunately the experiment, just like every other time man has wanted to play God, had its limits and downsides. Nowadays GMO's are a huge threat to public health and the environment. In June 2003 researchers at the Belgian Scientific Institute of Public Health (WIV) put thirteen negative issues concerning GMO's to the fore.

Meanwhile it has been shown that by growing GMO's extremely hazardous genes are developed in cultivated crops. The genes produce superviruses which will ultimately be absorbed by the gut flora. To put it briefly, this is yet another technology that we employ without giving it a second thought. But in spite of all these negative effects the agricultural lobby tries to persuade farmers to say goodbye to their traditional ways of working the land in favour of the promise of much higher returns.

This has had a disastrous effect in India. The so-called Green Revolution, introduced by the USA and supported by the World Bank, was meant to increase India's agricultural production by providing new cultivars, agrochemicals, and irrigation methods. Instead it led to an increase in suicide levels among farmers due to disappointing yields. Because they had bought expensive seeds, fertilizers and pesticides they were unable to pay off their debts.

Vandana Shiva

Quantum physicist and environmental activist Vandana Shiva has been fighting these despicable practices for years.

She is "the thorn in the side" of food giants like Cargill and Monsanto as she advocates biodiversity and ecological farming. She thinks that in the long run modern kinds of agriculture are detrimental as they are causing erosion of the soil. She backs up her story with results from an extensive study which shows that mixed agricultural land use produces more nutritional value per hectare, and causes less soil depletion.

In the 1990s she set up an organization called Navdanya, a female-focused movement for the protection of biological and cultural diversity, which is also referred to as the 'new gift' - a gift of life, heritage and continuity.

Navdanya is a network of seed keepers and organic farmers spread across seventeen states in India.

Vandana Shiva and her organization have collected indigenous seeds in various places in India. These seeds are strong, they grow using natural fertilization and don't require pesticides.

In this way, biodiversity and a badly-needed more varied menu is guaranteed. (From: NRC Handelsblad, the Netherlands, 19 August 2009). For more information, go to: www.navdanys.org.

This incredible courageous woman deserves a statue!

Fortunately the consciousness created by greater knowledge about health food is growing, and the supply and demand for organic food is ever increasing.

More and more people decide to grow their vegetables and herbs in their own garden or even on their own balcony. This is a very positive development.

THE WORLDWIDE DANGER OF ANTIBIOTIC RESISTANCE

Another alarming situation is the excessive long-term use of antibiotics in the livestock industry, and over-the-counter sales of these products, for example in India.

We are left with very few effective antibiotics to fight resistent bacteria. If we carry on like this we will turn back to medieval circumstances. We should take action swiftly, globally!

We need to change our policies: antibiotics should only be used to control extremely harmful, life-threatening bacterial infections. Effective natural remedies for viral infections exist, like echinacea, propolis and colloidal silver.

Because of the irresponsible use of antibiotics in intensive farming businesses (The Netherlands is a front runner using 5.5 tonnes a year, of which 80 percent is for cattle-breeding) all kinds of dangerous resistant bacteria have ended up in our food chain.

Additionally, the resistant bacterium MRSA regularly features in news bulletins.

In the Netherlands, pig farmer Eric van de Heuvel had to look for alternative farming practices as a result of his daughter being in need of heart surgery, which turned out to be impossible because she was infected with MRSA. He gave his pigs probiotics, as a result of which they developed excellent gut flora, and became so healthy they no longer needed antibiotics.

Great results have also been accomplished with garlic supplements that made the animals perfectly healthy, and antibiotics redundant.

Knowledge and experience concerning this successful approach to keeping livestock in prime condition needs to be passed on globally, for instance by means of a databank.

An international ban needs to be implemented on the use of antibiotics as a preventive measure against livestock illnesses, since we need to be extremely cautious with the scarce effective antibiotics we have left. This can be achieved by providing more subsidies to organic farming, which creates the best conditions to maintain healthy livestock, so that the use of antibiotics can be reduced.

This can be achieved by providing more subsidies to organic farming, which creates the best conditions to maintain healthy livestock, so that the use of antibiotics can be reduced.

In countries like Russia, Ukraine and Georgia, they developed an effective method to kill harmful bacteria by means of bacteriophages. A bacteriophage is a tiny virus that enters into the bacteries DNA and kills it. In the Dutch TV program 'Dokters van morgen' (Doctors of tomorrow) Antoinette Hertsenberg takes a Dutch diabetic patient with a dangerous infected foot that could be healed anymore because of antibiotic resistance. Under the threat of an amputation he went to the

Eliava Institute in Georgia, where his foot was healed with the bacteriophage method.

This method is as old as the existence of antibiotic but the regular medical science was not interested.

At the moment we have already 700.000 people in one year who died as a result of antibiotica resistance and they predict there will be 10 million people dying in the year 2050!

That means that the bacteriumphage method can save many lives and has no negative side effects like the antibioticum method, that kills beneficial bacteria in our intestines and weakens our immune system.

The efforts of the pharmaceutical industry have failed to develop new techniques and cures, because there would not be enough profit in it for them.

Again, this proves that financial interests are considered more important than the well-being of mankind.

I can't say this often enough: this is a global problem!

In India there have been reports about the phenomenon of highly dangerous superbugs. Yet in other countries ever more people in hospitals and homes for the elderly are living with multiple resistant bacteria. They are put in quarantine where they live a life of isolation. This kind of care is predicted to become impossibly expensive in the future.

But according to a Zembla documentary: "the price of cheap medicins" also the fact that big pharmaceutic companies as Aurobinda drain the waste of their fabrics in India direct in the rivers, raises the development of super bugs. Investigation found multi resistant bacteria in the water (and 260.000 fishes died).

After a penalty the situation improved in december 2017. On top of that they also exploit the workers who live in slums and receive only 80 euro each month.

Deadly MERS virus spreading out of control in Saudi Arabia, leaps to Egypt as global pandemic begins. Mike Adams Natural News April 27, 2014

It has long been recognized by intelligent observers that a global superbug pandemic is inevitable.

Humanity has created the perfect conditions for this: global nutritional deficiencies, weakened immune systems, high population density, high-speed international travel and systemic abuse of antibiotics by medical professionals. On top of that, we are dealing with the excessive long-term use of antibiotics in the livestock industry and over-the-counter sales in countries like India. (M.F.)

Drug-resistant superbugs like MERS (Middle East Respiratory Syndrome) are 100% immune to every conventional medical treatment in existence. There is no antibiotic, no vaccine, no drug and no treatment practiced by western medicine that can stop these bugs… and infections are deadly.

MERS-CoV has been detected in camels in Qatar, Oman, Egypt and Saudi Arabia, and is spreading alarmingly to other countries too. MERS is a severe acute respiratory illness with symptoms of fever, cough and shortness of breath.

Antibiotic Resistance Is Now Rife across the Entire Globe. A first-ever World Health Organization assessment of the growing problem calls for rapid changes to avoid the misery and deaths of a potential "post-antibiotic era". April 30, 2014 By Dina Fine Maron.

FDA Dangerous antibiotic-resistant bacteria and other pathogens have now emerged in every part of the world and threaten to roll back a century of medical advances.

That's the message from the World Health Organization in its first global report on this growing problem, which draws on drug-resistance data in 114 countries.

Drug resistance found worldwide, new drugs needed Posted: Apr 30, 2014 11:48 PM

LONDON (AP) – Bacteria resistant to antibiotics have now spread to every part of the world and might lead to a future where minor infections could kill, according to a report published Wednesday by the World Health Organization.

In its first global survey of the resistance problem, WHO said it found very high rates of drug-resistant E.coli bacteria, which causes problems including meningitis and infections of the skin, blood and kidneys.

The agency noted there are many countries where treatment for the bug is useless for more than half of the patients.

The WHO report also found worrying rates of resistance in other bacteria, including common causes of pneumonia and gonorrhoea.

Unless there is urgent action, "the world is headed for a post-antibiotic era in which common infections and minor injuries which have been treatable for decades can once again kill," Dr. Keiji Fukuda, one of the agency's assistant director-generals warned in a release.

It reveals that this serious threat is no longer a prediction for the future; it is happening right now in every region of the world and

Dr. Robert Becker, "The Body Electric," recognised a correlation between low silver levels and sickness. He said the silver deficiency was responsible for the improper functioning of the immune system. Dr. Becker's experiments conclude that silver works on the full spectrum of pathogens without any side effects or damage to any part of the body.

He also states that the silver is doing something more than killing disease organisms. It is also causing major growth stimulation of injured tissues. Patients with burns and elderly patients notice more rapid healing. He discovered that all cancer cells change back to normal cells. All strains of pathogens resistant to other antibiotics are killed by colloidal silver.

In his book: Positive silver kills all types of bacteria' he states: It works against all types of bacteria and viruses. In laboratory tests with colloidal silver, bacteria and viruses and fungal organisms are killed within minutes of contact.

All you need to know about colloidal silver

What makes Colloidal Silver so effective is the ionic charge that silver brings into the body.

Humans absorb it so rapidly, due to its small ion size, that it is absorbed by the blood before it can reach the gut. The micro-electrical (ionic) charge disables the particular enzyme that all one-celled bacteria, fungi and viruses use for their oxygen metabolism - its 'chemical lung'.

Colloidal Silver travels with the blood and enters the cells to seek out and destroy harmful organisms. Within minutes of the initial contact, the pathogen dies and is then cleared out of the body.

Colloidal Silver is absolutely nontoxic and safe for humans, animals and plants. The body does not build up a tolerance to it and studies show that Colloidal Silver does not form silver deposits within the body. Once Silver Colloid Water starts to work, destroying the invasion of bad bacteria and viruses with no side effects, the body gradually returns to normal and proceeds in creating its own anti-bodies. The British Medical Journal reports that it rapidly subdues inflammation and promotes healing. Dr. Robert Becker noticed a correlation between low silver levels and sickness: colds, flu etc. A single virus will invade a living cell within the body tissue. Then, the insidious pathogen will take over the nucleus of the cell and alter its production and reproduction mechanism to replicate the virus instead of the enzyme, hormone or other chemical the body would have otherwise produced for itself within that cell.

"Colloidal Silver is known as an immune enhancer. Silver works by disabling the oxygen-metabolizing enzyme that one-celled bacteria, fungi and viruses use to reproduce themselves. The disease-causing pathogen therefore suffocates and dies and is eliminated via the normal channels.

Resistant strains have never been known to develop, unlike antibiotics which are effective against only about a dozen forms of bacteria and fungi, but never viruses."

Later, the newly produced virus will be released from the cell into the bloodstream. However, another very interesting phenomenon takes place. As the virus affects the cell for its own purposes, part of the response of that living cell is that it reverts back to a more primitive form of cell structure and chemistry. The oxygen-metabolizing enzyme, or chemical lung in the cell wall, reverts as well.

"The use of modern man-made antibiotics has increasingly led to mutant strains of germs that the antibiotics can no longer kill. Colloidal Silver does not appear to have this problem. Why? Because unlike man-made antibiotics which are basically "bug poison for the human body," Colloidal Silver is not a poison. Instead, it deals with all germs in the same way: it suffocates them by disabling the enzyme they need for respiration."

This more primitive form of enzyme is vulnerable to the effects of Colloidal Silver.

The catalyst effect of the Colloidal Silver simply being in close proximity to the enzyme of this cell results in the enzyme becoming permanently disabled. It cannot function to bring oxygen into the cell and the virus-producing cell dies by suffocation.

Dhyana Coburn is the co-author of *The Wonders of Colloidal Silver*.

In a separate article entitled "Colloidal Silver – A Healthy Silver Lining" she adds more information on the mechanism by which Colloidal Silver interacts only with harmful microbes:

- "Colloidal Silver kills invading microbes by dissolving an enzyme that metabolizes oxygen in primitive organisms. The process is an electrochemical reaction. The cell cannot breathe, suffocates and dies. That's why it works on all types of germs, including the super-germs. Metallic and chelated minerals carry a negative charge but colloidal bioelectric minerals carry a positive charge. Therefore, another way for Colloidal Silver to inhibit germ growth is the positive charge on the Colloidal Silver (particles) binding with the negative charge of the pathogen. This causes an interruption of the biological function of the organism, which then cannot reproduce."

A careful and thoughtful approach towards the prescription of antibiotics on a global level is of vital importance. This type of medication must only be used in cases of severe illness or infection.

There is still a lot of ignorance: when suffering with flu and even cold symptoms, many people ask for antibiotics, while colds and flu are mostly caused by a virus. Antibiotics are intended to fight only bacterial diseases.

Colloidal Silver remedy kills both bacteria and viruses.

I take a standard dose of Colloidal Silver on a daily basis in order to protect myself the best I can against the 'invasion' of all kinds of viruses. In case of a cold or the flu, I raise the dose. The remedy can also be used for animals. In Tuscany I have four cats and whenever one of them becomes sick, Colloidal Silver helps them recover, for instance from respiratory diseases. It is also a wonderful remedy to heal damaged skin.

ABOUT THE THREAT OF TOXIC CHEMICALS

On January 26 2006, I made a press statement on the damaging effects of agricultural chemicals. At the time, scientific research had pointed out that one bunch of grapes was seen to contain 13 different types of agricultural chemical. This is more than enough reason to worry, since only a small amount of chemicals can cause endocrine disruption. Dr. Tinka Murk, toxicologist, has stated that it is a combination of chemicals that causes health risks, even if individually they do not reach the official limit.

We are continually exposed to all kinds of chemicals without being informed of the risks, even though the damaging effects have already been long-proved by animal testing. Besides, this fails to address the fact that chemicals are tested individually, while we are being exposed to a multitude of these chemicals at the same time.

Most people do not have a clue about the amount of dangerous chemicals around us, threatening our health at this very moment.

One dreadful example is the softening agent used in plastics which causes endocrine disruption.

In their famous book *Cradle to Cradle* Braungart & McDonough offer us substantiated criticism on the current large-scale industrial system, and point out the health risks resulting from the high level of stress we are exposed to and the dangerous chemicals destroying our immune systems and damaging our cellular and hormonal processes.

Approximately 80.000 chemicals and technical blends are currently being used. Only 3.000 of these products have been investigated and labelled as safe for living organisms.

A Dutch television series called Zembla showed an alarming documentary revealing the serious risk of endocrine-disrupting chemicals. It pointed out that researchers have come up with sufficient evidence that all kinds of chemicals including pesticides, plasticisers, cleaning products and even parabens in cosmetic crèmes are damaging our health, and are very dangerous for unborn babies.

Many cosmetic and pharmaceutical products contain parabens as a preservative.

A recent Danish investigation showed that people who used a lotion containing parabens on their skin had traces of parabens in their blood and urine some hours later.

Toxicologists throughout the whole world have raised the alarm and pointed out that exposure to this kind of chemical could even lead to permanent brain damage. They advise all future mothers to stay away from these toxins. Their advice is to eat organic food and to use 100% natural cosmetics and cleaning products and detergents. In addition they recommend us to stay away from canned food since the inside of the cans contains the toxic Bisphenol A. In France this substance has recently been banned.

In 2003/2004 The National Health and Nutrition Examination Survey found detectable levels of BPA in 93% of 2517 urine samples from 2517 people aged six years and older.

Proof that toxic chemicals, including certain pesticides and solvents, are the cause of the increasing amount of neurodevelopmental disorders among children, like autism, attention deficit and hyperactivity disorders, is increasing. Philippe Grandjean, endowed professor in the field of environment and health, and Philip Landrigan, chairman of the faculty of global health published their research findings online in the 'Lancet Neurology' in February 2014.

There is another chemical substance named glyphosate that can cause cancer, changes in our DNA and also great harm to our environment.

It is available in shops and garden centres under the name Roundup, the famous, globally used product of the multinational Monsanto, to fight unwanted weeds. People spray it on their terraces and then let their children play in their gardens without any notion of the danger. But it also causes problems in agriculture: glyphosate stunts the growth of roots and the assimilation of water by crops.

Despite the fact that in Germany traces of glyphosate have even been found in mothers' milk, Rukweid, 'das Forum Moderne Landwirtschaft' (Forum for Modern Agriculture), denies everything. Cancer experts of the World Health Organisation (WHO) are frustrated by this denial. Glyphosate pollutes our ground water and consequently also our drinking water. Consumers should immediately cease buying Roundup and seek out more environmentally friendly substances. Beside the dangers of these toxic products to the consumer and the environment, there is also danger to the workers who take part in the production process. In a Zembla documentary it was seen that the business-concern 'Du Pont' used the dangerous substance p.f.o.a. (C 8) as an ingredient for the production of Teflon as a non-stick layer in frying pans. There are female employees with severe health problems and there was even mention of the birth of deformed babies in America. Thousands of people are waging juridical war against Du Pont and are gathering evidence in order to fight back.

This company has also committed crimes against the environment by disposing of harmful waste in river systems. I hope this war will be ended soon with an impeachment and a conviction including the payment of compensation to the victims for the harm and grief they have suffered.

We seriously haven't got a clue about what else we are facing and which 'invisible enemies' are still out there.

A Dutch news channel revealed that a type of fungus has been discovered in the air we breathe. Its spores, called aspergillus, can penetrate the body via our lungs. 500 to 600 patients a year are said to be affected by this fungus, and one patient a week dies from the symptoms.

It is not yet fully clear how this fungus came into existence. It has, however, been discovered that pesticides, especially antifungal agents, paint and wood treatment products play an essential role.

The World Health Organization drew up a comprehensive report on this global threat and 89 scientists appealed to the EU.

It is a fact that the number of premature babies, boys with undescended testicles, men with weak sperm counts and men with testicular cancer is continuously increasing. Furthermore, the number of women with breast cancer is increasing at an alarming rate, especially in The Netherlands, a country with the most polluted air in Europe.

In Denmark, they refused to wait any longer for the further research that would be necessary for a ban on certain chemical agents and decided to use the precautionary principle instead, to ban for instance the dangerous parabens themselves.

They started a major information campaign especially addressing pregnant women, advising them to protect their embryos as well as they possibly can. These women are recommended to stick to a mainly organic and varied diet, use natural make-up and skin products and avoid aggressive, chemical cleaning products as much as possible. The Netherlands however are being hesitant, and still make their decisions based on economic interests.

Countries like Denmark, using the precautionary principle, and Germany, with their 'Energiewende' ('energy transition'), are an important example to the rest of the world but we - and I mean all citizens of the world - should become aware of the fact that:

Chemical pollution will only be reduced if consumers collectively start living a sustainable life, and vote for green political parties.

The manufacture of harmful and environmentally damaging products should be reduced where possible and we should return to the 'old' familiar sustainable alternatives. Before the Industrial Revolution, none of these chemical products existed. Cleaning agents, paint and weed control were all produced or performed in a natural way. I remember going to The Hague when I was 25 years old to buy paint based on natural ingredients. I went to Amsterdam to buy toys manufactured in a natural way. When I was 30 years of age, I had a fulltime job as a higher vocational teacher. I went to live in the countryside and tried to live in the most natural way possible. We ate vegetables from our own garden and drank homemade elderflower and elderberry wine. I even cooked on an antique wood burning stove using waste wood from the forest. We never used any pesticides or fertilisers. We had our own compost heap and I made fermented stinging nettle water to control aphids.

This may sound very complicated but it is actually very simple. 'Mother Nature' always knows what is best for us. If you let nature take its course, you will discover an abundance of edible plants, fruit, seeds and roots in your surroundings to keep you alive. This is the way our ancestors lived and yet all their precious information about edible crops is at risk of being lost forever. Today I still use only natural products for my make-up, skincare, clothes and cleaning products. I only eat organic food, not just because it contains more micronutrients for optimum health but also because mainstream supermarket food contains harmful additional matter like synthetic colorants and preservatives (the so called E-numbers).

In Tuscany, I have a dear friend called Dagmar, one of the best herbalists I have ever met. One day she fell off her horse and was seriously injured. In the hospital they provided her with steel ribs, which solved part of the problem. However, her lungs had turned into 'minced meat'. She managed to cure her own lungs using ancient herbal medicine.

In Tuscany, we celebrate Befana on January 6. Together, we make a big fire and write down our pain and grief on little notes, which we then burn in the fire. Afterwards, we celebrate life and eat dishes prepared from the crops grown directly around Dagmar's house. Up to 10 kinds of lettuce with a delicious fragrance are waiting to be harvested and enjoyed!

We need more of these rituals strengthening the bond between humans and nature.

I am aware of the fact that not everybody is able to live in the countryside. However, anyone is capable of trying to live as healthily as possible.

THE NEGATIVE EFFECTS OF GLOBALIZATION

Globalization has caused a tidal wave of employee dismissals and has increased the workload for those who remain. This has resulted in increasing numbers of people who are exhausted and burned out. At the present time family relationships are under a great deal of pressure and more and more young people are unemployed and going off the rails. Inner turmoil and worries about the future lead to a craving for addictive substances and domestic violence is increasing.

We also see an increase in random acts of violence, driven by boredom and the feeling of an inner void. Depression is threatening to assume epidemic proportions and we see more and more people who are so financially desperate that they see no other alternative than to end their lives.

David Stuckler has since 2008 been investigating the impact of the harsh cuts to public health systems in 54 countries.

He has written a book on his conclusions, called *The Body Economic: Why Austerity Kills*. He discovered that there has been a clear increase in infectious diseases, heart attacks, depression and suicide, amongst other things.

In the Netherlands alone the number of suicides has already risen by 20 percent since 2008, and in the southern European countries the number is even higher.

He goes on to criticize the policies in countries such as the Netherlands which result in severe healthcare cutbacks at the very time that more and more people are developing physical and mental health problems. Because of this, society is pushed even further out of kilter.

In recent years in the Netherlands we have seen severe cuts in the budget for specialist psychiatric help, which has now been put into the hands of family doctors.

We are currently seeing almost daily new reports of horrific incidents of people going berserk, such as attacks on innocent civilians out walking with their dogs, or recently on a woman who was delivering newspapers on her bicycle and nearly died because of her injuries.

There was also a report of a man who went on the rampage, breaking the windows of a number of houses and destroying several cars in the same street. He left a shocking trail of destruction until he was finally overpowered by five policemen. Reports of cars (or houses) being set on fire are frighteningly regular.

It is remarkable that these incidents often happen in small towns where life used to be so peaceful and quiet. Stuckler shows us there is another way to proceed.

In Iceland the government invested 20 percent more in health care during the last financial crisis, in order to support the Icelanders as best they could and help them through the crisis.

Ashcroft's critique on our current economic system

Ross Ashcroft made an interesting film called 'Four Horsemen' which clarifies the negative consequences of our current economic system. The compulsion he felt to make this film began several years ago. Ashcroft: "Around the year 2006, we realised things in the financial industry were completely messed up. Some excesses were incredibly corrupt and intolerable. So you sit there, watching one of the biggest robberies in history taking place, and there are two options; either you sit back and let it happen, or you decide to do something about it. I realised the economy is too important to leave it all up to economists."

He started an investigation which revealed that neoclassical economics as taught in the major universities doesn't even come close to reality, since the current economic ground rules only encourage us to achieve progress by destroying the planet.

"In our current Western world we are put into a 'consumption coma' and people are starting to realise that we only need 'less', and that a simple life is a great life".

We are dealing with an unimaginable level of human suffering, especially in developing countries. Speculation on raw materials has become the main source of income for investment banks. Goldman Sachs alone makes a net profit of nearly 5 billion dollars every year, purely on commodity derivatives. A civilised society should no longer be putting up with these kinds of people and operations. Major change and reforms are needed! It is our job to help the people who are suffering from this silent torture.

Speculation on food and other basic needs has to stop, since it increases food prices and makes the people of Africa and other countries suffer even more.

In addition, we need to establish a tax system which enables people to enjoy the resources of their land. If we receive oil and diamonds from Africa, then these people should be sufficiently rewarded, in order to allow them to build proper road networks.

Far too few people are aware of the causes of this huge level of suffering. The main media organizations are now owned by the insurance and real estate industries, who don't want people to discover what is really going on since the amount of money they make depends on the level of ignorance of the people. This has got nothing to do with a conspiracy theory; it is simply the cruel economic reality.

The moment has come where people can no longer tolerate the pain and the nightmare, but this increases our hope that people may actually start to take action!

The most important step we can take is to set up our own organisations and institutions, like cooperatives, in order to develop skills with people at a local level and build strong communities. All such initiatives show a rise in the happiness index.

It is the current structure that pushes us towards rivalry and destruction.

As soon as this structure is removed, the wish to co-operate will easily surpass the need to exploit and destroy one another. Many people say human beings act like wolves, which isn't true at all. Wolves do not eat each other, they support one another!

This is why Ashcroft continues to be optimistic about the future. "We will suffer, we will make mistakes, but in the end we will make it. This is a more exciting era to live in than ever before!"

For more information, please check out:

www.fourhorsemenfilm.com

www.renegadeeconomist.com

Or read the book *Four Horsemen: The Survival Guide Manual* Motherlode, 2012. Source: Share Nederland, March 2013

While I totally agree with Ashcroft, I would like to add that the only way to reverse the current process is for enough people to wake up and be willing to take action.

EXPLOITATION OF EMPLOYEES IN THE 3RD WORLD

Today, the exploitation of employees has become even worse than ever. Major multi-nationals have moved their production processes to Third World countries, where people are being exploited and even abused on a very large scale.

We seriously have very little idea of the cruelties that take place there. What we do know is determined by the limited horrific images we see in the news, or in documentaries on specific scandalous situations, like factory accidents and the abuse of girls, hired by the companies that make up our Western textile industry, in countries like Bangladesh. Instead of exploiting Third World countries the government should help businesses to learn how to produce in a sustainable way in their own country, in order for the economy to grow and to reduce unemployment.

But all too often the opposite happens. A documentary by Zembla showed how in The Netherlands since 2000 we have seen a shift in development aid from **aid to trade**.

For instance:

- In Ethiopia 130 businesses have been established using
  €200 million in subsidies from the Dutch government,
  but these businesses are not obliged to provide details
  about their trade results to the Chamber of Commerce.
- The Heineken company received €6.6 million to take
  over two national breweries in 2011, but the modernizing
  of these breweries resulted in 699 people losing their
  jobs.

Many more harmful practices are now being caused by the unashamed exploitation of the local population by Western businesses.

For example, another Zembla documentary showed how the Dutch company Barnhorn, whose assets are around €200 million, propagates 3.5 million roses per day in East Africa.

The cultivation of each rose requires 7 liters of water which is extracted from the local lake and river as well as being pumped out of the ground. Moreover, this company is accused of dumping chemical waste in these same water supplies. This causes severe problems and hardship for the people who live in the region, but that is not all; the employees themselves are also being exploited.

The average rose picker receives just €29 per month - even less than the earnings of a textile worker in Bangladesh. Even so this company, which goes under the name Sher, carries the Fair-trade logo! **How is that possible?**

Similar problems take place everywhere, such as in Nigeria where China and France have involved themselves for a while in the uranium business before leaving with the profits.

One final example of how current policies are failing: At present 10 million Ethiopians are threatened with starvation by the ongoing drought. An emergency fund of €9 million was established, offering - with the help of Cordaid - emergency relief in the form of water and medicines. Each family received only 20 liters of water to last four days, but this help could only be offered until May 2016 after which the money had already run out.

These problems are not limited to Ethiopia; they occur in many other African countries too, including Eritrea and Angola which are also suffering erosion due to climate change. We must not forget that the rich countries with their irresponsible, materialistic lifestyles are the main causes of these problems.

All these examples clearly demonstrate that subsidies to businesses offer no guarantee of a dignified existence for the local population.

If there comes no end to all these exploitation practices, then even more refugees will be fleeing towards Europe. Western developed countries should help third world countries to set up their own sustainable production units, for instance by providing microcredits.

MICROCREDITS TO FIGHT POVERTY

The United Nations have made an urgent global appeal to help fight world poverty, and this appeal has been heard by the international community. Provision of micro-credits will be the centrepiece of the UN Campaign. The first bank to integrate micro-credits in its policy is the Grameen Bank in India. Founder Muhammed Yunus won the Nobel Peace Prize for his 'efforts in order to create bottom-up economic and social developments'. To achieve this, the Grameen Bank deployed local credit organisations, since they know the people and the local circumstances well.

The poorest people, earning less than 1 euro a day, were provided with loans in order for them to build up their own little businesses. In addition, they were offered training and technical support for starting up these businesses. One of the conditions for receiving a microcredit is participation in a weekly meeting with their microcredit provider. This allows the microcredit provider to verify whether or not the agreement on the loan repayment is being respected. The huge success of microcredits has been shared and shared again. It enables people, especially women, to make their own living and to look after their family and children properly.

Women make up two thirds of the world's estimated 1.5 billion 'extremely poor' people. In addition, women have been shown to be more reliable when it comes to paying off their debts than men. The microcredit campaign – the Microcredit Summit Campaign – resulted in many microcredit programs. From 2004 until 2006, microcredits were provided to about 22 million people, including 12.5 million of the poorest people in the world.

The target was 39 million people in 2006, which is actually a long way from being enough, considering the aforementioned figure of 1.5 billion extremely poor people living on this globe.

250 million people worldwide have received microcredits according to the ING report. Microfinance makes a difference!

In the meantime the amount of people with microfinance is much higher since the outcome of that report.

The Dutch **Anne-Marie Rakhorst** deals with this issue in her book *Duurzaam ontwikkelen... een wereldkans* (which means:

Sustainable development... an opportunity the world must not miss).

Among many other wise words, she writes the following:

"We can't change the world on our own, we need each other. This means we are all jointly responsible for the improvement of the living standards in developing countries. In that sense, the results of microcredits were to me impressive. Men, and especially women, setting up their own business with a 50-euro loan. For them, this is a huge amount of money and they have to deal with the debt. However, this money and the support provided by their financiers enables them to build their own future and to escape from poverty and to send their children to a decent school, since without education they will end up nowhere.

Microfinance and fair trade will not bring universal happiness. However, they can be the stepping stones to a better life. The wealthy Western World has to support this process. And fortunately it does. Currently, microcredits are an integral part of the policy of trendsetting companies in this field, Triodos and ASN, and recently also Rabobank, ING and ABN Amro. The dutch queen Maxima has become a figurehead of the microcredit system. Her passionate pleas at countless gatherings encourage companies to join the microcredit club. She is the perfect ambassador to point out its huge importance to anyone who will listen."

GROWING RESISTANCE AGAINST EU'S PRIVATISATION POLICY

The highly informative documentary 'Catastroika' by Katarina Kitidi and Aris Chatzistefanou shows how the European Trojka is guilty of bad practices by forcing European countries to hand over basic services to commercial organisations or, in other words, the market force. In my view, this procedure is totally wrong: citizens pay taxes to the government in order to safeguard basic services including the provision of food, healthcare, education, housing, electricity, public transport etc. However, although we have continued to pay taxes over the past decades, the government is handing over more and more of our basic services to commercial organisations, giving these profit seeking businesses the power to decide whatever they want regarding our basic services. This process is being gradually realised in a silent and secretive manner.

After the fall of the Berlin Wall, Mr. Treuhand was responsible for the DDR privatisation, and consequently for the fate of 4.5 million labourers. Political parties were bribed to stimulate privatisation.

Many businesses were privatised with great speed, and many were closed if this was considered beneficial to the West German economy. The end result was that there were only 1.5 million jobs left, the Gross Domestic Product (GDP) dropped and the unemployment rate rocketed from 0% to 20%.

Mr. Juncker used the DDR privatisation model as an example for Greece and a fund was founded with 3 members appointed by the Trojka, who laid down strict conditions. A group of Greek business people and officials stayed in the extremely expensive Claridge hotel to discuss the sales procedure for Greek institutions.

Picture the scenario: external forces decide that the Greek infrastructure needs to be privatised, a process that will be monitored and managed by foreign multinationals.

It sounds very similar to an occupation, or a classic example of Neo-colonialism where the citizens' basic human rights, as laid down in the UN Universal Declaration, are being violated. In Greece - where the very principle of democracy was founded - international, political and financial power blocs (the so called 'bankenjunta') have led the democracy to its own destruction. And this doesn't just happen in Greece.

In England, the rail transport privatisation resulted in an abject failure that has led to 42 deaths and 500 injured people so far. In France, President Chirac handed over the Paris water service to the commercial power companies Veola and Suez, whose executives also belong to the International Monetary Fund (IMF) and are related to the European Central Bank (ECB). A clear case of conflict of interests! After the take-over, prices increased enormously. A group of ecologists then successfully took back control over the water services, and the prices dropped again.

In Italy, a referendum relating to water management was held in which the Italian population voted against the privatisation of their water. This vision was honoured until the new interim government came into power - a government led by bankers like Draghi. They made sure the privatisation became reality in the end, and this resulted in sky-high water bills. Another case of democracy being trampled underfoot.

Portuguese household water bills have also risen excessively and the people who have already been hit particularly hard by the financial crisis are now being pushed to the point of exasperation. It is just another example of the despicable practices that we need to fight if we are to prevent things from becoming even worse.

Conclusion: at first, privatisation may lead to small profits. In the long run however, greater losses will be the result as it leads to fewer jobs and an increase in energy costs, health insurance premiums etc. This reduces the spending power of the people and leads to growing insecurity amongst citizens.

I saw an interesting episode of the critical Dutch TV programme Radar, featuring Antoinette Hertsenberg. After undertaking thorough research, she concludes that Greece was 'fiddled' into the European Union. In order to be admitted to the EU, the national debt of a country cannot exceed 60% of the Gross Domestic Product. In 2001, Greece's national debt was 150 billion. Fiddling the books and currency swaps helped Greece get into the EU: loans at low interest rates were seen to be no problem whatsoever, but when the financial crisis started to kick in things started to go badly wrong. National debts were increasing fast and Greece, threatened with bankruptcy, lied about its financial situation before Papandreou was finally forced to admit that the actual debt was much higher than claimed. Hertsenberg believes that Northern Europe has made a huge profit from the Greek debts. She states that it is absolutely intolerable that Greek citizens have to suffer as a result of the major mistakes of political leaders, bank lobbies and businesspeople. 30% of the Greek population are unemployed. 72% of this group are young women! There is no unemployment benefit system in place and half of the healthcare system has fallen apart. One of the sad examples of the consequences Hertsenberg mentioned was the case of an unemployed man who was forced back to living with his elderly mother again. Together they had to live on € 420 a month. The poorest people are now having to scavenge for leftover food in the bins, and desperate people are trying to escape reality by using cheap chemical drugs.

THE GREEK PARALLEL ECONOMY

Some years ago a major revolution took place in Greece, driven by the massive economic crisis: a parallel economy has been set up which sidelines the middlemen and allows the people to take control of supply and demand. Volunteers were organising citizens' movements all over the country. It all started in Katerini, where people started selling potatoes directly to the consumer for one third of the retail prices. The major success of this initiative encouraged other people to take action, such as rebooting a local washing powder factory and starting to make cheese out of their own milk etc. The enormous power and success of the movement made several administrators decide to support their activities. Mr Boutaris, mayor of Thessaloniki wanted to facilitate these initiatives and Mr Tsipras, then a leading presidential candidate, gave lectures all over the country in order to encourage this development.

His words were: "We need to regain the right to live in this country".

People were fighting to keep control of their water supply. Members of one of the citizens' movements set up the '136 movement' in which each member deposited € 136 in order to buy out the water company. However, their offer was turned down. Suez, a French company, was aiming to buy the company but the movement submitted the case to court. They were worried that the water quality would not be guaranteed and that a major increase in the water price would ensue. Tsipras' left-wing Syriza party supported the movement. I am unaware how this process ended but citizens' initiatives to take control of basic services always make me happy. Greece teaches us that we cannot change the world on our own, but together we stand strong.

Mr. Alexis Tsipras, who won the presidential elections, is currently trying to reverse the privatisation established by the Trojka (initiated by the European Commission and the International Monetary Fund). For example: Greece was being pressurised into selling the Thessaloniki and Piraeus docks to China. Initially it looked as if they were managing to keep hold of the docks through their efforts. The dockworkers were overjoyed and started working twice as hard. Unfortunately, I have since heard that Greece has now been forced to sell the docks after all. Tsipras is trying to evade the heavy debt burden by means other than the forced reforms and austerity policies now in place. He wants more time for the Greek population to take a deep breath and get back on their feet, as they are severely suffering from poverty and bad healthcare, and are actually in the midst of a severe humanitarian crisis.

He wants to fight corruption and fraud and deal with the rich people who have safe-guarded their money in foreign countries. I am eagerly following this process and wonder whether he will be able to keep his promises. Unfortunately, he is being forced to increasingly meet the Trojka's demands. He is dealing with an incredibly heavy political inheritance and his country has gone bankrupt. The majority of the Greek population have withdrawn their savings from the banks. People are afraid that, without yet another loan, there will not be enough money to pay their wages and pensions. The last years Greece was still facing a deep crisis and the IMF had proposed that the European Union must remit a part of their debt. According to the latest news the Greek economy is running better as a result of severe economic measures, but many Greek people still suffer from poverty like before.

Regardless of the final outcome for Greece, one thing is clear: a new era has started. more and more people want to take control of their own basic services, including in Northern Europe.

To all the Northern European countries pointing their fingers to southern countries while blaming them for messing up, I would like to say: You could also change your perspective; people in Southern countries know how to enjoy life and to live in the moment, while people in northern countries, driven by the old Calvinistic attitudes and impregnated with materialistic values such as greed and an obsession with possession, work at such a high pace and raise the pressure so high that more and more people suffer because of a burnout from work stress and from the new diseases of affluence.

And of course corruption and fraud crimes are committed in the north of Europe too; the difference is that it is done in a more subtle and underhand way.

Every time I watch a documentary about people in 'less developed' countries who have dinner together, gathered around a fire, singing together while someone is playing the guitar, I can't help thinking they are happier than we are. We are glued to our couches and our computers after a long day of work. Or we go out for dinner 'together' while we check our mobile phones more often than we do the faces of our friends and family. In spite of all our gadgets and gizmos we never seem to be satisfied and we never stop looking for more. Driven by our crazy schedules, and feeling the pressure of sharing our bright and shiny lives on Facebook, depression has become the number one epidemic and the number of suicides is increasing at an alarming rate.

In the meantime the amount of protests was rising. Pablo Iglesias of the Podemos Party in Spain had managed to mobilise tens of thousands of people who have completely had it with the policy of Mariano Rajoy of the 'Partido Popular'.

The Greek Syriza Party is also worth a mention: it has a genuinely revolutionary vibe which comes across as: "Podemos – Syriza, we are walking side-by-side". In Italy the 'Cinque Stelle' party of Beppe Grillo is growing every day. Members put a part of their salary into a fund which lends it to people in need of money. Peaceful revolutions and passionate speeches fill me with joy. Quotes like: 'I have a dream' by Martin Luther King or song lyrics like James Brown's 'Say it loud, I'm black and I'm proud' or Bob Marley's 'Stand up for your rights' have resulted in an increasing level of awareness and self-confidence amongst the black population.

During the Arab Spring, protestors were occupying the squares night and day to fight for their democratic rights, whereas we let our governments gradually take away our rights one by one. So far, the protests in Europe have been mainly confined to Southern Europe and the only movement that stirred itself for quite a while was the Occupy Movement. It really surprises me that, so far, people have not revolted en masse against all the unscrupulous practices taking place.

Fortunately, on 9 February 2016, a new movement for Democracy in Europe (DiEM 25) was founded to fight against the technocracy. Many activists who support DiEM 25 are inspired by the vision of the Greek professor in economy, Yanis Varoufakis.

Citizens must hold their governments accountable and take action if they fail in their primary tasks. As a way of political punishment, citizens should stop voting for political parties that are supporting unscrupulous lobby groups, in order to loosen the hold that these parties have on society.

In this respect, too many people are still unaware of the vital issues and lack the necessary understanding.

Let me get this straight: the government should ensure that the quality of our basic facilities is guaranteed, since this is one of the main reasons we pay taxes. But we see everywhere that they step back and extradite us to commercial institutions.

In fact, the bureaucratic infrastructure of our industrial world is way too big, it is non-transparent and unnecessarily complicated. We are trapped in a suffocating web of unnecessary rules which make our lives more difficult.

Accountants, solicitors, lawyers, judges etc. - especially in their written work - use language that is too complicated for most people to understand.

However, I believe that the days of neoliberalism, governed by market forces, are numbered because all around us there are battles taking place. Battles between the short-sighted, destructive powers of former materialism and a new, constructive force of a growing global movement that has

simply had enough of the pseudo-democracy we live in and aims to reform our society in a way that regains our control over our basic facilities.

On the other hand, we are also now seeing strong signs of nationalism and fear of foreigners arising on a huge scale, and populist political parties are growing rapidly. In Europe we are seeing growing numbers of adherents to leaders such as the Dutch Geert Wilders, the French Marine le Pen and the English Nigel Farage etc. And now that the despot Donald Trump rules America, every day signing harmful decrees (to take measures against global warming and against regulation of the bank-sector etc.), we can clearly see how afraid and angry the people who vote for these populist leaders are. It also demonstrates a lack of consciousness and insight into the real causes of our huge global problems.

There is a great danger that Fascism will rise again and the worst example we see in Europe is the repulsive Neo-Nazi party "the golden dawn" in Greece. They use openly Hitler symbols and their leader, Nikolaos Michaloliakes spent even 18 months in prison.

We see everywhere that people are placing the blame for our real problems on the shoulders of refugees and migrants. This is very shortsighted: the real blame has to be laid on the multinational lobbies of the old school, who use employees as paws in their chessplay. They discharge them from their jobs and they transfer their companies to low-wage countries in order to gain maximum profits, while they commit tax-dodging practices on a large scale. On the other hand we can put the blame on all governments who don't take enough care of their most vulnerable inhabitants.

FAILING REFUGEE-POLICY OF THE EUROPEAN UNION

Nowadays we are faced with the influx of an unbelievable amount of migrants in Europe. The European politics fails because Europe is not able to monitor the external borders. It is incomprehensible to me how shortsighted and incompetent the refugee policy has been until now. It is heartbreaking to see how an unnecessary number of people drowned and the ones that arrive have to contend with a lot of problems. In North Europe they get bored of doing nothing. In Holland they are often transported to other shelters which has a negative effect. Specially those that came from Syria or Iraq suffer from mental health problems because of traumatic experience.

Especially in Italy the situation is distressing, I am a daily witness. In the autumn of the year 2016 there arrived thousands of refugees coming from Libya on a daily basis. There are even days there arrived 5000 refugees.

Although the Italians show an unbelievable devotion in the reception centers, there is also bitter grief in southern Italy where refugees have been exploited by the mafia with the employment in the tomato harvest. They live in self-made huts of a few shelves and a frame of plastic and I saw interviews where they told that this suffering was worse than the life in Africa. They cannot leave Italy because the borders in the north are hermetically closed.

In the meantime minister Marco Minniti signed an agreement with the Libyan coastguard which resulted in a decrease of 26,6% refugees. Italy also made an agreement with Frontex that they are no longer obliged to bring the saved crowd to Italy. Joanne Liu, president of "Doctors Without Borders", visited Libya and declared that the fact that most of them are brought back to Libya causes an indescribable suffering. We knew already that they were mishandled put in prison or sold as slaves. But the reality is even more horrible: at 18.2.2018 we saw a Youtube fragment where refugees were loaded in a bus and sold to be killed for the sale of their organs. The record was made with the mobile telephone of one of the victims who implored to spread this horrible news out over the world. But the next day it was removed from Youtube.

In Greece we saw heartbreaking scenes as the little boy who has drowned and was found on the beach. Also at the moment a tremendous suffering takes place on Lesbos where a great amount of refugees are suffering under the extreme cold weather in camps of tents. They are forced to stay there because of the doubtful deal that Europe signed with the Turkish president Erdogan. The EU paid milliards of euros to keep the refugees outside of Europe. It is unbelievable that the refugees in Lesbos are forced to suffer from cold and disease.

Also in Paris you find fugitives who are suffering from cold and hunger in tents on the banks of the Seine river.

Europe should take care immediately of these poor people and bring them to a warm and dry reception centre. It irritates me to death that some northern European politicians, like the Dutch Mark Rutte, claim with smugness that the refugee issue is now resolved. How is it possible that they close their eyes for the suffering of refugees in Italy and Greece!

According to a Dutch documentary of Tegenlicht (which means 'Backlight'), Europe signed an agreement with Nigeria to stop the influx of migrants in exchange for one billion euro. Agadez was the junction of passenger traffic were African people of the southern countries came together to find smugglers of migrants.

The intention of the European Union is to create a big barrier between Nigeria and the southern African countries to stop the migration to Europe.

The journalist Ibrahim Diallo reports that there is a severe control to pick up migrants on their way to Libya, keep them detained and send them back to their homeland. The smugglers risk years of imprisonment that's why there remains a kind of dubious type of smuggler, people that are willing to take this risk and use secret, dangerous roads in the Sahara-dessert.

In the meantime many dead bodies of migrants are found in the sand, like Diallo showed with photos on his telephone. This sad tragedy shows once more how important it is to give realistic information. Migrants often have a total wrong image of the reality.

I saw a group of migrants hidden in a house in Agadez and one of them said: 'In Europe you find easily work and then I can take care of my family'. This idea was based on a television fragment he saw when he was five years old.

Wake up! As migrant you get stuck in Italy and 40% of the Italian youngsters is unemployed and many of them leave Italy to find work in Northern European countries.

There is only one durable solution: The explosive, harrowing situation in North Africa has to be resolved by means of international intervention.

The United Nations should have the power and competence to intervene in war conflicts and stop suffering and bloodshed.

The Western world contributed to the chaos in North Africa. Bush and Blair made dramatic mistakes by starting an illegal war in Iraq and failed to create a save infrastructure after the fall of Saddam Hussein.

The same applies to Libya where an enormous chaos was created after the death of Gaddafi. This power vacuum created a hotbed for the jihad in the manifestation of Al Qaida and many others and the last years the horrific Isis-movement.

As long as the situation in North Africa remains atrocious the borders of Europe have to be controlled better. I am an opponent of open borders and in my opinion the European Union made a big mistake to open their borders, because you give criminals and terrorists a free entrance in Europe. Europe has to dissolve more than enough problems since the big economic crisis of 2008.

In the southern European countries 30 to 40% of the young people are unemployed. There are more and more poor people who rely on the food-banks.

If countries cannot provide food for their own people, there is only shelter for refugees coming from war-zones like Syria, Iraq, etc. There is no place for economic migrants or fortune seekers.

At the moment we see a mixture of these types of refugees in Europe and when the permission to stay of economic refugees is refused a part of them is so frustrated and angry that they cause annoyance or even become criminal. If they are finally banished from the country they go into hiding. Sometimes the country where they came from refuses to take them back. As a result of all these problems there is less care for the deeply traumatic refugees from the war-zones, like women and specially the vulnerable young children.

The European union most take immediate care of these victims of war that are forced to stay in Greece and Italy and bring them to other countries in Europe. Every country has to take a part according to the amount of inhabitants. It is not possible that the Balkan-countries refuse to take them and leave Greece and Italy alone with this immense burden.

There must be payed more attention to extensive information-campaigns in Africa about the different kind of problems the economic migrants have to face. The chance that they will get a permission to stay is nil, so after their life-risking crossing the sea (There were 4.500 drowned in 2016) and all sorts of hardships they have to suffer, they finally have to return to their mother-country. In a state of disenchantment they regularly escape and live on hiding in a clandestine existence.

We see in many big cities in Italy, in Rome, Milan and Genua how they often live under horrific circumstances, like we see in the documentary of the Dutch writer: Pfeijffer who lives in Genua, where a man from Gambia sighs: "If I had known everything before, I would not have come to Europe". But there is also a film-fragment of the Dutch television program: 'POW' were you see an integration project where a Syrian refugee had to visit an 'old people's home' where a group of women made Christmas decoration. He tried his best to make one, but some of them gave him criticism. At the end he said: 'I don't know what is worse the war in Syria or sitting here'. He said it in such a dry way that it was tragic-comic..

On the other hand there are of course also well integrated refugees.

But there is also a very dark side of this problematic process:

1. First of all there are male migrants who are not used to live in a free European society where the women are liberated and behave themselves in a free way and dress themselves in the eyes of these men too sexy. We have seen what happened in Germany between Christmas and New Year in Cologne where many women were molested and palpated.
2. Second of all, clandestine migrants who are hungry risk to be tempted to criminal activities like stealing, or drugs-dealing.
3. Third of all, and this is the worse-case-scenario, among the refugees you find also radical Muslims, with the intention to commit terroristic attacks in Europe.

The end-conclusion is that by the arrival of all these migrants there has to be a quick but profound shift of, the real 'war-refugees' and the 'economic refugees'.

For the war-refugees there must be a shelter, but for the economic refugees there is no place as long as Europe refuses to divide them honestly.

It is inadmissible to leave Italy and Greece alone with this huge problem while all the neighboring countries closed their borders.

Moreover, European refugees who want to turn back to their motherland because they are appointed with their life in Europe, have to receive all help possible and their motherland countries have to be forced to take them back. There are countries like France who succeeded in negotiating with Morocco for a return program.

THE CREDIT CRUNCH AND THE DYSFUNCTIONAL FINANCIAL SECTOR

Thomas Piketty

In his bestseller *Capital in the 21st century*, **Thomas Piketty** shows the significantly increasing income inequality since 1980.

This book has been translated into 28 different languages and his lectures draw large crowds. He consulted dozens of experts in 20 countries and discovered that 60% of the total capital is owned by only 10% of the population. And this difference will only get bigger since the capital of rich people is growing 3 to 4 times as fast as the capital owned by other people. The middle class pays more taxes than the rich people and the extremely rich escape tot their tax havens. Middle class people are suffering under extreme pressure and private debts keep on rising.

No surprise, considering we are living in an unsustainable and very vulnerable financial system." Piketty states that a broad European movement should be established and social scientists should take a stand against this inhumane system. In addition, citizens should organise a social platform in order to put pressure on politicians.

Wealth taxes should be raised, labour taxes should be reduced

The level of secrecy in the banking industry is higher than within the CIA, and is not checked by any democracy or whatsoever. They do whatever they choose to and their extreme power is undermining democracy and creating a 'finacracy' instead.

According to scientists Richard Wilkinson and Kate Pickett, income inequality causes all kinds of problems including an increasing crime rate and a growing amount of mental disorders.

In Michiel Vos and Alexander Pelosi's documentary 'My America' we see how a young generation in the internet industry becomes extremely rich within a short period by creating all kinds of digital masterpieces, also known as 'disruptive innovation', since they are capable of destroying existing businesses with their inventions. Currently, these 'kids' are settling down in San Francisco in luxurious skyscrapers that are built all over the place. These new billionaires gradually chase away the original residents who sadly watch the new developments unfold. It is painful to see how some of the hard-working older residents go downhill. A sad example is Allen, who, after being fired, was forced to sell everything he owned because these people have no right to any kind of long-term income supplements. Today, he lives in a tiny little room in a complex, sharing kitchen and toilet with other residents sharing the same fate.

His words are, and I quote: "The American Dream does not exist. For most people it has turned into a nightmare."

GROWING RESISTANCE AGAINST FAILING GOVERNMENT POLICIES

The government is supposed to monitor and manage our basic services and social security system including the quality of our food, housing, education, health care, working conditions, transport facilities etc., and a transparent financial infrastructure. However, and I repeat it again: the government is dramatically failing to do so! They force us to pay taxes while leaving us at the mercy of market forces.

A growing number of people has had enough of our governments' failure to supervise large institutions that look after the interests of citizens and who are responsible for the quality of our everyday surroundings. As a result, the banks were given free rein to speculate with our savings, and to sell ambiguous and risky products getting their customers into financial trouble. This is called deception and fraud and normally such dubious practices are punished, but in this case the banks that went under and dragged people into the current financial crisis were saved by the government (and this is still going on, for that matter). This means that taxpayers are paying the price for bad banking decisions. This is why we should strongly oppose these scandalous and unacceptable practices. History has taught us that large-scale institutions are much more difficult to supervise, and as a result too many managing directors are busy lining their pockets even further at the expense of staff members. An increasing number of fraudulent activities and corruption scandals are coming to light.

The bureaucratic regulation is stifling and is a heavy burden for people who are running their own business.

If we refrain from action the financial sector will destroy the world's economy and pose a threat to our democratic values.

There must be more supervision on banks. Their scandalous practices were shielded by accountants and auditors who were implicated by approving annual reports of failed banks. In other words; they are guilty of falsifying figures.

Maleficent accountants come up with complicated methods to help multinational corporations channel money through letter box companies to tax havens in order to evade taxes. The Netherlands plays a large role in these practices. This particular tax avoidance strategy is called 'Double Irish with a Dutch Sandwich'. Member of the European Parliament, Eva Joly has been expressing her concerns about this construction for the last years. She demands more transparency from the EU because our current tax system is unjust: The system overburdens the lower incomes and the working class while letting off the wealthy scot-free. Joly now hopes that the citizens of the EU will revolt en masse against these practices. In a Dutch television program called 'Rambam', hidden camera videos recently revealed multinationals throughout the whole world negotiating 'secret' deals with the Dutch Government.

The NFIA (Netherlands Foreign Investment Industry) explains the Dutch government how to help businesses to evade taxes when settling their business in the Netherlands.

According to Rambam, 24.000 companies have already settled their businesses in the country, of which 4.000 reside in the 'Amstelgebouw'.

As long as this kind of malicious and unscrupulous practices are not being dealt with, social turmoil and outbreaks of violence as a result of income inequality will increase throughout the whole world.

A Zembla documentary shows us that moreover third world countries loose a lot of income because of the Dutch so called 'letterbox companies'. By way of these trades they let flow in and out untaxed money.

Although these companies are legal constructions that were created in the past to favour the interests of the multi-nationals there is a huge wave of criticism on the policy of tax-paradises like the notorious Cayman islands and others. Tax havens should be severely punished for their crimes. In his days, Ronald Reagan gradually reduced tax rates for the rich from 70 to 50, and finally, to 35%. Today, rich people only pay 15%. If the rich pay this little tax or dodge the middle class stagnates, budget problems will arise and democracy is being undermined. The recent revelations of the extent of tax havens in the 'the Panama papers' and recently the 'Paradise papers', will hopefully, finally put an end to these evil practices. Nevertheless it will be very difficult to fight against these tax-dodging practises because they are so widely ramificated.

For instance in 100 business trades in London with a stock-exchange quotation have 8000 subsidiaries in tax-havens.

Joris Luyendijk

In his book, *Dit kan niet waar zijn* which means: "This cannot be true", the Dutch writer Joris Luyendijk describes how in September 2008 the bankruptcy of the US Lehman Brothers-bank introduced a global credit crisis by which our society was deeply disrupted. How could this happen? Luyendijk describes it as follows: In the years before consumer banks and mortgage lenders specially in America and England, have lent too much money to ordinary citizens, especially for mortgages. As a result the housing prices were inflated tremendously.

The mortgages were sold to investment banks, divided in pieces and repacked, into increasingly complex financial products, which were bought by pension funds and other investors.

The US insurance giant *American International Group* (AIG) insured many products and credit rating companies and gave them even a triple-A-status. The products were becoming more complex and many banks held a share in their own old holdings without good financial buffers and non-transparent structures in tax havens.

At a certain moment millions of homeowners, especially in America could no longer meet their financial obligations and the "dubious" financial products fell heavily in value or exploded and became worthless.

Investors were forced to take their losses and banks had to write off the damage and the question was whether their buffers were big enough and for the Lehman Brothers bank they did not have these and went bankrupt. This created a domino-effect of distrust and in a short time nobody in the financial system was willing to lend money to each other. The authorities had to dig deep in the treasury scan and the Central Banks showed further decline in interest rates and pumped large amounts of new money in the system.

In this way the global credit crisis was born and today we are still suffering from the consequences.

Finally the ordinary taxpayer had to pay also for the mistakes that were made by the banking system. At the moment the cold is not yet out of the air.

Luyendijk states that a cloud of fear is floating above the London financial centre. The financial industry is seriously ill, and few has changed since the last financial crisis. In his eyes, the knowledge of the bank staff is too fragmented. They all carry out their own activities without fully understanding the whole process. It's as if everyone is fitting in their own little piece of the jigsaw. If, for instance, someone faces a problem while checking a computer program, his or her supervisor often hasn't got a clue how to solve it. Non-transparent systems lead to more profit. Tricky derivatives are still sold and the whole system is still rotten and corrupting towards humanity. Bankers often don't even understand their own balance sheet reports and still too many bonuses are granted.

After the financial crisis of 2008, the banking system should be reformed but it did not happened enough.

There are still given too often fat bonuses and there is always a danger of a new credit crises and if that happens again the consequences are incalculable, because there are insufficient buffers.

Finally there is even a risk that the whole financial system will collapse. There is an urgent need to take effective measures to reform the bank sector.

Roberto Savio, founder and chairman of the Inter Press Service (IPS) news agency, states that the banking industry no longer serves the economy. Instead it focuses on serving its own interests.

Financial transactions are currently totally 40 trillion a day, compared to an economic production of 1 trillion a day.

Besides corrupting the political system and carrying out illegal activities (bringing in billions of dollars), the banks are currently mainly financing the big investors, making it impossible for smaller businesses to get a loan.

The efforts of Mario Draghi, chairman of the European Central Bank, to provide credits to small businesses and private persons have largely failed. (Source: Share Netherland, March 2015.)

Draghi decided to reduce interest rates and to pump instead of 60 billion euro's, 80 billion monthly in the European economy.

This policy will benefit the Southern European countries that can borrow money easily without enough emphasis on the need for reform. Therefore there is a lot of criticism from Northern Europe because their pensions will come under pressure.

Sustainable reform of the banking sector

In the future the main hub of the financial market will most likely be located in China. In 2015 China launched the 'Asian Infrastructure Investment Bank', which now has even more capital than the World Bank. This new bank is acquiring an increasing number of members, amongst them the UK and Germany. America is not amused; their debt has increased by billions. The financial market is unstable and according to insiders a new financial crisis of unequalled proportions is looming.

There is an urgent need for a great clean-up of the system. New banks must be established which engage themselves in the provision of transparent financial services to their customers, and which invest only in a new, sustainable economy.

I advise everyone to change over to small-scale, sustainable banks such as for example the ASN bank and the Triodos bank in Holland.

But there are many others like the Brac bank in Bangla Desh, specialized in micro-finance or the Vencity bank in Canada. More information you find at the Global Alliance for banking on values: **gebv-org.**

At the moment we see a positive development: The world of big money is receiving increasingly more demand for investment in sustainable, green energy. The cost of green energy even fell recently below the costs for the fossil fuel sector. In fact there are now so many potential investors that there are not enough green projects available for them.

The tipping point has been reached, and the pension funds are also receiving ever more demand. The well-known Warren Buffet recently decided to invest in wind and solar energy projects, and in Dubai a press conference was recently held in which the importance of further development of sustainable energy was underlined. In China the solar energy branch is also developing at lightning speed. They strive to be world leader.

THE CLIMATE CRISIS IS OUR GREATEST THREAT

There is another danger that will affect all of us in the near future; the current, ongoing climate crisis is like a ticking time bomb. We have poisoned our planet with incredible amounts of chemical and nuclear waste and destroyed a big part of our beautiful nature. We are increasingly ruining the ecological infrastructure and we do not realize that we are ruining the roots of our existence. Ever since the foundation of the Club of Rome, climate scientists have been warning us for the dangers of the global warming. But too few people seem to be aware of the gravity of the situation.

They predict the sea level will rise and the climate of the northern countries will be too cold and wet, while the southern countries will dry out due to a lack of rain. This will lead to millions of climate refugees.

There is an enormous lack of awareness of the dangers of climate change among large sections of the population.

Powerful lobbies of certain multinational companies, banks and investment trust funds have been causing the greatest part of the damage. They have huge interests because of their exorbitant profits. Because of their power, they have too much influence on international politics, national governments and media. They even infiltrate universities and by doing so they undermine value-free science.

Science should be neutral and based on facts but they regularly spread false information on global warming and try to discredit natural medicine. They invest in huge advertising campaigns to encourage people to consume as much as they possibly can. So far, they have been very successful indeed; we strongly depend on their products. It is not even possible to quietly watch television nowadays, since we are continuously terrorized by stupid commercials.

Many people feel frustrated and powerless, and sigh about not being able to create change all by themselves. But if we join forces we can make a difference together and force lobby groups to change their policies. We will get control of our own lives if we take our basic facilities as much as possible in our own hands.

The danger of a slowdown of the Gulf Stream

Since the last few decades, the Arctic ice is melting and large amounts of freshwater are flowing into the Arctic Ocean. This might have a catastrophic impact on the temperate climate in Europe and North America.

The Gulf Stream originates in the Gulf of Mexico, flows in between Cuba and Florida and further northward. The decreasing salinity in the oceans threatens every climate balance in the temperate zones; it changes the currents and may keep the Gulf Stream from flowing which slows down the arctic water.

This is an ongoing process with a monthly increasing effect and the disaster resulting from it may occur much sooner than we think; a slowdown of the Gulf Stream has already been measured. This means the phenomenon is already a fact and the only questions to which scientists haven't got an answer is when the breaking point will be reached which will put a permanent end to the flowing of the Gulf Stream.

This is a very dangerous development and although this fact is also confirmed in a secret report of the Pentagon, most people are not informed.

A dramatic vicious cycle

Submarines underneath the arctic ice have measured a 40% decrease of the ice sheet. Today this decrease is even worse!

The melting of the permanent ice sheet resulted in a vicious cycle with a snowball effect since the ocean in the form of water absorbs more solar energy than ice, which is characterized by reflecting most of the solar energy. This phenomenon increases the warming of the water, making the ice melt even more, and so on and so forth.

A similar phenomenon occurs at the Siberian and Canadian permafrost; as the snow layers shrink, the earth will start to absorb the sun rays instead of reflecting them.

This results in a warming of the permafrost. Methane will be released (with a far more significant greenhouse effect compared to CO_2), increasing the global warming.

According to the latest alarming research – carried out by NASA, among others – the permafrost on the Northern Hemisphere appears to be melting much faster than anticipated. The amount of past methane and carbon dioxide emissions is so great, that we are probably too late to limit the greenhouse effect to 2 degrees Celsius.

If we continue with our current lifestyle, all the ice of Greenland, and part of Antarctica, will melt and the sea level will rise 6 to 7 meter.

THE RISKS OF A SUDDEN CLIMATE CHANGE

As Mark Serreze, researcher at the Colorado University, says, 'The Arctic is changing fast. Our concern needs to be focused on the fact that it is happening right now and that we need to adjust to this change.'

The climate change as a result of the end of the Gulf Stream may happen very suddenly. The most recent measurements reveal that this change may occur very soon, most probably before this century has come to an end. This makes it easy to imagine that this ocean conveyor belt will have completely disappeared within fifty or even twenty years. In that case the surrounding countries will become significantly colder.

This phenomenon may trigger other phenomena, which might end up in an incredible global disaster: in our areas, we would enter a new age similar to the ice age and the tropics would move southward. It is presumed that 40% less rain would fall in the humid areas like the Amazon in Central America, which would change the ecosystems and transform the tropical rain forest into vast prairies, while in the Asian countries the monsoon will no longer exist.

The drought may result in a lower methane concentration which makes the temperature drop even more.

World hunger would increase, causing anxiety (resulting in millions and millions of people trying to escape) which will most probably be fatal for our economies. (From: *Demain la Terre*, Yannick Monget)

We're already witnessing the appalling effects of climate change in the shape of extreme cold, drought, heatwaves, heavy rainfall and violent storms, hurricanes, whirlwinds, and even typhoons.

How many natural disasters do we need before mankind wakes up and starts to live responsibly?

When will we finally realize that we should respect and protect our planet's ecological infrastucture, because it is the foundation of our existence!

I will repeat once more: large parts of the population show an enormous lack of awareness of the dangers of the climate change. Although it has become very clear that our ignorant and wasteful methods of production and consumption have significantly contributed to the greenhouse effect, to such an extent that ice sheets and glaciers are melting at an alarming fast pace, we prefer to remain silent and to put our heads in the sand. Only a small part of the population is willing to take action.

This to me is unbelievable. How in heaven's name can so many people close their eyes for all these alarming messages on the climate catastrophes we are facing?

"People, wake up! Change your lifestyle and put pressure on the government to take the necessary measures."

I have been taking action and been protesting for 14 years. With every climate congress, I have been trying to find an opening to break the deadlock. I was extremely irritated when not enough participants of the climate congress in The Hague turned out to be willing to help reduce the CO_2 emissions with 5% within ten years (not even close to what it should be).

Below, you can read what I wrote about it in 2000: November 23

URGENT REQUEST TO ALL VISITORS OF THE CLIMATE CONGRESS

As a psychologist and writer I have to express my big anxiety about the ominous results of the greenhouse effect.

I consider this as the biggest threat of actual human life on earth. Every right-thinking person on earth will understand that drastic measures are required to prevent farther escalation, and what do I see?

An enormous lack of consciousness and responsibility

Three years ago, the congress in Japan ended with the intention to reduce the expulsion of CO_2 with 5% during a period of 10 years.

Although this percentage is much too low because 60-80% is required, till now only +/- 27 countries did ratify this intention.

And in the meantime the polar cap is melting more and more. It's obvious there has to happen much more:

1. All directions of all top-industries in all welfare states must be put under great pressure to eliminate the expulsion of CO_2 as much as possible. They must be forced to spend a part of their million and milliard profits to save our planet.
2. It is necessary to create severe laws to protect our environment and severe punishments towards environment criminals.

A permanent international 'supervision' committee with extreme competence has to be developed as soon as possible.

1. The research to create clean fuel for cars has to be PRIORITY NR. 1. The interests of the big oil companies are of minor importance.
2. Public Transport has to be elaborated considerably and has to be made far more attractive and much cheaper.
3. The production of wind and solar energy has to be increased as much as possible. The research to develop other forms of clean energy will be of the most importance.

I will end this request with a personal intrusive question to all men and women in power:

Do you realise that you have direct power to save our planet? If you don't use this power you should be very ashamed about your behaviour because in that case you saddle up your children, grand-children and the whole mankind with the inheritance of an unscrupulous capitalism.

WE HAVE TO TAKE BACK THE CONTROL OVER OUR LIVES.

We are not powerless, but we have given too much control over our lives away. So we need to take this power back.

The all important breakthrough in creating a healthy and happy life will only come if a majority of people wakes up and decides to buy sustainable organic products, switch to renewable energy and small-scale facilities have been established that operate out of fundamental needs instead of financial gain.

We need to be really convinced that our present way of living in the industrial countries is based on the destruction of nature, and the fact that we are marching towards our own doom fast.

Now we have to learn to protect what is left of nature and we have to give mother earth a chance to recover from the incredible damage done by us.

This will involve a financial investment. However, if we stay as neglectful as we are now, the price will be so much higher.

For years I have been pointing out the importance of a worldwide committee of extremely competent and wise people (whose hearts and minds are connected) with far reaching authority, enabling them to take drastic measures.

Fact is, national and regional authorities mostly are not capable of establishing an effective, durable, integrated policy.

Some measures require a long-term planning, such as cutting back on dangerous nuclear power and changing to sustainable kinds of energy. Other measures to protect our oceans and rain forests can be realized sooner. We have to consider this protection as our number one priority!

WE HAVE TO PROTECT OUR OCEANS AND PRECIOUS CORAL REEFS

About 75% of the earth is made up of seas and oceans but we seriously polluted this magical, magnificent underwater world. Large-scale fishing methods cause overfishing, damage the seafloor and disable local fishermen to make a decent living. On top of this, dynamite fishing techniques seriously damage the colorful coral reefs, the incubator of the fish stock.

1/2 of the beautiful 'Great Barrier Rif' in front of Australia is damaged because of the rising of the temperature of the seawater as a result the algae on the riff are dying and 40% of the sea-animals are dependent on this sea weed.

And last but not least, we caused enormous pollution dumping incredible amounts of plastic, chemical and nuclear waste. Jean-Michel Cousteau has been warning us for years: 'As a result of man's use of fossil fuels, a thin layer of oil now covers most of the ocean's surface, choking the microscopic life that is the base of the food chain, changing life at the most basic level. We have very little time to reverse what we have been doing and minimize our effect not just on the ocean but on the entire natural system. It's quite frightening' (source: OCEAN, Boyce Thorne-Miller).

Research done by Tara Oceans revealed that large parts of our oceans contain high levels of plastic particles. This is damaging for algae, sea plants and marine animals, and eventually also for humanity.

Fact is that marine life, especially plankton, helps us fight CO_2 emission by absorbing it, and produces 50% of our oxygen through the photosynthesis process.

The enormous 'plastic soup' slows down this process and reduces the oxygen level. Besides this, the marine animals are absorbing toxins including bisphenol. Toxins that we absorb, when consuming these animals.

Recent deep-sea research in the Mariana trench which is considered as an untouched area showed that on a level of 10 kilometers deep, there was a huge concentration of harmful substance. This investigation mentions a chemical combination in little lobster-type sea animals and these chemicals are very difficult to break down. In the meantime there are everywhere minuscule parts of plastic as well in the mussels and oysters as in our beer and even in the honey and this is very alarming news.

According to the latest survey by the world wildlife fund half of the fish population and other sea creatures has already disappeared.

Research WWF 16 September 2015:

Life in the oceans over the past 40 years is alarming.

The fish populations, marine mammals, reptiles and sea birds in and around sea are dropped by an average of 49 percent.

Fish stocks of species who are worldwide much eaten, such as tuna, are even collapsed with three quarters. In addition, the surface coral, mangrove forests and sea grass fields greatly diminished, while those areas act as nurseries for the sea.

This is stated in the Living Blue Planet Report that the World Wildlife Fund (WWF) released internationally on the 16th September. The oceans special edition of the Living Planet Report appears just before the United Nations approves sustainable development goals against poverty before the end of the month. WWF calls on Member States to protect and restore the oceans to give an important role therein.

A large part of the population, mainly in poor countries, depends on their food and income on a healthy sea with sufficient fish.

There should be a ban on overfishing with mega fish trawlers and fishing methods like trawling that destroy bottom life, or worse damaging the coral reefs with dynamite.

WE HAVE TO PROTECT OUR PRECIOUS RAIN FORESTS

We have to make sure the destruction of the rainforests will stop for they are an essential part of our ecological infrastructure and they contain valuable medicinal plants. What's more, they convert carbon dioxide into oxygen which reduces the CO_2 emission.

The Western demand for tropical wood causes major problems. Every year, a surface of The Netherlands of tropical woods disappears worldwide. That means every second the size of one football-ground. And the consequences for the local population are simply harrowing.

The European timber regulation against illegal logging entered into force on March 2013. However, these rules will only be effective if compliance with the regulation is intensively monitored.

I have been a member of the *Nederlandse Milieudefensie* (which means: Dutch Environmental Defense Fund) for years. This organization is planning to establish a structural monitoring program which allows them to punish illegal loggers immediately.

All over the world, these unscrupulous men destroy our precious nature and the lives of countless human beings and animals.

An eyewitness of the 'Nederlandse Milieudefensie' gives expression to the suffering of farmer families in Cameroon:

"I just couldn't believe the way the timber companies were ruining large parts of Cameroon and literally destroyed the lives of farmer families, day after day, after day. 14% of all the cut tropical wood we use in The Netherlands is from Cameroon. An essential part of this wood is still being cut illegally today. I spoke to Kanga and Françoise. You can hardly imagine what they are

going through. The illegal cutting of wood <u>severely deprives them and many other families with young children of food and drink.</u>

Bulldozers ruining plantations unannounced

Kanga and Françoise have to make their living from the vegetables they grow on the small piece of land next to their little farm.

Kanga hunts in the woods in order to be able to feed his family sufficiently and to make some money for medical care by selling what's left.

Many families depend on this extra income to send their children to school.

A timber company established a major logging track using heavy bulldozers on the land of Kanga and Françoise, without any prior notice. A major part of their fruit plantation was destroyed without offering any form of compensation. The trees are now cut in no time. On top of this, poaching becomes more common as a result of increasing poverty, hence the territory of rare animal species is becoming smaller every day." (Source: Milieu defensie / Friends of the Netherlands June 18, 2012)

It is staggering that there are people who cut down these treasured rainforests for construction of palm oil (or soya bean) plantations, while there is enough land elsewhere in the world to build such plantations. This should be prohibited!

Abhorrent practices are taking place in Indonesia. Large tracts of tropical rain forest are deliberately burned by unscrupulous environmental criminals.

In Sumatra the smoke – which affects the air in Malaysia – was so suffocating that people had serious health problems because of a lack of oxygen.

In Pekanbaru the State of emergency was declared. A large number of orang-utans had to be evacuated in Borneo. There were animals that were covered with burns. The local inhabitants scream for help, but the Government is doing NOTHING!

Because the mighty palm oil lobby has bribed the local authorities so that they can burn down the precious rainforests unhindered, forests that provide a wealth of medicinal plants and which through the process of photosynthesis CO_2 eliminate emissions.

I feel so much anger that my blood boils. This needs to stop.

I urge everyone to put pressure on the Indonesian Government to put an end to these disgraceful criminal practices.

Yesterday night I saw the documentary: 'The Borneo case', and it blew my mind: This docu shows there is an international financial network of holdings, offshore-bank accounts, etc., with a annual turnover of 30 billion dollar to support the infrastructure of the corrupt rainforest–destruction industry, and there is lots of money laundering. The Goldman Sachs Bank lend out money, but the Deutsche Bank and the Dutch RABO, ING, and ABNAMRO banks are also involved.

With the help of this dirty network Taib Mahmud, minister of forestry could enrich himself with the destruction of the biggest part of the beautiful rainforest of Sarawak, and build up a fortune of 15 milliard.

It was impressive how a small group of brave people did everything possible to save the rainforest in Sarawak, like Bruno Manser who 'disappeared', and the local Urud Mutang who travelled around the world to, talk with world leaders, but ... unfortunately ended in the prison where he was also tortured. After his release he went to Canada and decided to turn back to Sarawak to save the remaining rainforest.

Together with Clara Brown he started 'Radio Free Sarawak' in London.

Finally they succeeded with the help of the Swiss Lukas Strauman, to investigate the evil practice of Taib who owned real-estate all over the world and at the end he resigned and his successor Satem Adenun announced a prohibition to fell trees and the shutdown of the building of a big barrage.

This was a huge victory and all the people who risked their life to save the rainforest are heroes and we need more of them!

We have to exert our utmost strength to stop the destruction of our precious rainforests.

Greenpeace want to save the trees who assimilate the highest amount of CO_2. In the so called 'High Carbon Stock-Projects', Greenpeace works together with Indonesia to measure with the help of a satellite which trees have to be saved, but that is not enough all trees have to be saved!. This is good news, but there is also bad news: There is an enormous development of the so called BIO-MASS and they call it unjustly: sustainable energy. In Holland they use bio-mass in the coal power plant.

They act as if the expulsion of CO_2 by the wood of the bio-mass is not so bad for the environment. There is even a subsidization available of three and a half milliard euro for the coming eight years.

According to chemical specialist Martijn Katan the consumption that burning of biomass does not produce CO_2 and can be considered as source of sustainable energy is not true, on the contrary: In a Zembla documentary we see that only a small part of the bio-mass consist of the rest-waste out of the paper- and furniture-industry, but for a big part they have to chop woods. Because there is little wood left in Holland they have to import other wood out from the Baltic States or from America for instance from the mighty 'Industrial Pallet Association'. They defend their policy always in the same way: 'We do not only chop woods, but we also replant woods'.

The 'Dogwood Alliance' gives specific criticism: They chop old precious woods with a big bio-diversity where all kind of animals live, and they replant leafless fir woods.

THIS DOES NOT HELP REDUCING THE GLOBAL WARMING BUT MAKES IT WORSE!

It is unbelievable - and I say it again - how blind mankind is for the danger of global warming which, according to the Meteorological Institute of the United Nations, takes place much faster than we assumed.

Consumers should decide to buy wood and paper with the fsc label, and avoid products containing palm oil.

ANNIE LEONARD'S PLEA FOR LESS CONSUMING

Leonard is part of an extensive global community of people who feel that something is terribly wrong. Our economy is in disarray. Half the world's population has less than 2,50 dollars to spend a day and cannot afford their basic needs, while a small elite few rakes in an obnoxious amount of money. Our industries turn our planet's natural resources into wastelands by emitting poisonous chemicals at such an omnipresent scale that these substances can be found in every human body, even that of a newborn baby.

Still our Western culture encourages us to find solace in unbridled consumerism, instead of compassion and commitment.

Leonard, who spent twenty years researching international waste trade and worked for Greenpeace, released her documentary "The Story of our Stuff' in 2007. The film was a massive online hit. She asks the viewers to carefully consider about what to buy.

She says that according to research our feelings of happiness won't increase when we reach a certain level of consumerism, but decrease instead. We grow less happy because we need to earn ever more money to be able to buy all those coveted items. This in turn impedes our social and familial ties.

Her campaign is based on raising a new kind of awareness that faces what consumerism does to us, our fellow human beings all over the world, and the earth itself.

When we're able to understand this, we will also realize that we need to establish a new culture of sustainability and reduced consumerism in which people matter more than products.

Her solution is threefold:

1. We have to change our worldviews, and redefine the meaning of progress. Instead of measuring progress based on gross national product (GNP) we could employ the Index of Sustainable Economic Welfare which measures the amount of raw materials and levels of pollution. Or an even better one, the Happy Planet Index (www.happyplanetindex.org) that compares

environmental impact and human wellbeing. This principle is already implemented in Bhutan! (M.F.)

2. We need to ban war. How come there is always enough money to start a war while relief for those in need is of lesser importance? Instead of keeping spending money on warfare we should invest more in healthcare, education, and renewable energy.

3. We should value time over stuff. Shorter working days are good for our health, plus they improve social wellbeing and reduce stress. A reduced level of consumption has less negative impact on the environment. It is said that our economic system will collapse when we work and buy less, but Leonard refers to a number of economists like ecological economist Hermann Daly, who claim that a gradual reduction of working hours and consumerism will give us a chance to adapt the economy to a slower pace without much problems.

For more info surf to: www.storyofstuff.com From: **Share Nederland**, no. 5, June 2010

Remember Ghandi's famous quote:

THE WORLD HAS ENOUGH FOR EVERYONE´S NEED, BUT NOT ENOUGH FOR EVERYONE´S GREED

Besides Annie Leonard, more people have made films and documentaries in order to point out the fatal consequences of our current economic system for humanity and the environment. We all know the impressive film 'An Inconvenient truth' by Al Gore which informs us on the climate disaster that is happening right now. An accompanying book was also published. And this climate warrior never stopped trying to wake us up and give us hope for the future, proven by his recent article:

Positive signs emerge everywhere

Fortunately, also positive signs emerge from both the business world as well as from the international governments. As Al Gore states in his article: 'The turning point: new hope for our climate.'

- Electricity generated by photovoltaic (PV) solar panels is available for the same or a lower price than electricity from other sources in more than 79 countries. The more these panels are being used, the lower the price will become. In Bangladesh, for instance, two new solar panel systems are being installed on roofs every minute. This turns Bangladesh into world's fastest growing market for solar panels. An explosive growth is also expected in West and East Africa.
- China revealed to be capable of generating 70 gig watt of solar energy in 2017. Xi Jinping, China's president, has banned all new coal-fired power plants in several cities, and forces all big industrial enterprises to have their CO_2 emission registered
- China and the USA jointly agreed on curbing another seriously polluting source, the HFCs, short for Hydrofluorcarbons. India's new president revealed world's most ambitious plan aiming to accelerate the transition to solar power generation.
- Since 2015 there have been worldwide wind energy installations with a nominal capacity of 486,7 GW, which means 3,7% of the current supply. There is often resistance because people consider the ugly windmills as horizon-filthiness. But there are also beautiful ones like

the windturbine on a roof in Chicago, a project of Bill
Becker.

All these technological, business, economic and political trends
seriously suggest a break with the past. They actually provide us
with realistic hope for a solid road to resolve the climate crisis.
(Sources: rollingstone.com; grist.org)

United Nations Secretary-General, Ban Ki-Moon (chairman of
'The Elders', a group of independent leaders who are committed
to peace, justice and human rights on a global level), invited
world leaders of financial, business and social organizations to the
climate top on September 23 2014 in New York to generate
political commitment to a meaningful legal agreement. He
explains: 'Our job is to convert the biggest collective challenge of
humanity today – **climate change** – into the biggest chance of
jointly progressive steps towards a sustainable future. Members of
'The Elders' are striving for the world to be carbon-neutral by
2050.

For more information you can check www.theelders.org.

Demonstrations and events against climate change are planned all
over the world. Environmentalist Bill Mc. Kibben writes:

'This is an invitation. An invitation to anyone who'd like to prove
to themselves, and to their children, that they give a damn about
the biggest crisis our civilization has ever faced.'

On the organizers' website (peoplesclimate.org), we read:

'Our demand is for Action, Not Words: take the action necessary
to create a world with an economy that works for people and the
planet – now. In short, we want a world safe from the ravages of
climate change.' (Source: **Share Nederland**, September 2014)

Fortunately, also positive news of significant symbolic value from the business industry can be shared, including the Rockefeller Group in the USA announcing no longer wanting to invest in oil and coal.

They no longer think this contributes to a better future and are switching to investments in renewable energy. They joined a platform of 800 other green investors.

More and more countries are willing to contribute to a sustainable future; France has announced to deposit 1 billion Euros in a green fund aiming to support Third World countries.

I heard that the G-7 gathering in Bayern also resulted in another step forward. Credits go to Angela Merkel, who was trying her utmost to convince as many countries possible to agree on a maximal temperature rise of 2 degrees Celsius.

The G-7 leaders have already agreed. It is of vital importance that many other world leaders follow their example and I was really happy that finally a consensus was reached during the climate conference in Paris in 2015 to work together to realize this important target.

WE HAVE TO LOOK FOR A SMART ENERGY MIX

Priority number one is that we should make more use of renewable energy, and we should find alternatives for petrol and diesel.

We have to look for a clever combination of alternative energy sources such as nuclear fusion, hydrogen, earth-warmth, wind, solar cells, etc.

These renewable energy sources will at first supplement but in the long term replace fossil fuels. This involves all kinds of energy consumption: in transport and logistics, and industrial and domestic use.

Nuclear fusion: the utterly safe and clean alternative

The sun is one big nuclear fusion that has been producing heat and light for millions of years. This technique fuses nuclei with lower masses into denser ones whereby a huge amount of energy is being released. Fusion power is the safest, most reliable, and cleanest alternative for our future power supply.

Unlike with nuclear energy there is no chain reaction that can run amuck. With nuclear fusion only a few grams of fuel are put in the reactor for a few seconds of nuclear fusion to take place. For the nuclear reaction to stop you simply cut off the fuel supply. Fusion power emits no greenhouse gases, only harmless helium. Deuterium and lithium serve as fuels. During fusion tritium is formed out of lithium.

If you combine a deuterium and lithium atom helium is produced by the reaction, resulting in a neutron plus the above mentioned huge amount of energy. (Source: *Smart Energy Mix* KIVI NIRIA) From: *Duurzaam ontwikkelen... een wereldkans*, by Anne-Marie Rakhorst.

However, there are adversaries because it is a costly and complicated method.

Skunk works reveals compact fusion reactor details.

Lockheed Martin aims to develop a compact reactor prototype in five years, production unit in ten.

Oct 15, 2014 Guy Norris, Aviation Week & Space Technology

Fusion Frontier

"Hidden away in the hidden depths of Skunk Works, a Lockheed Martin research team has been working quietly on a nuclear fusion energy concept with the potential to meet, if not eventually decrease, the world's insatiable demand for power.

Dubbed the compact fusion reactor (CFR), the device is conceptually safer, cleaner and more powerful than much larger, current nuclear systems that rely on fission, the process of splitting atoms to release energy. Crucially, by being "compact," Lockheed believes its scalable concept will also be small and practical enough for applications ranging from interplanetary spacecraft and commercial ships to city power stations.

It may even revive the concept of large, nuclear-powered aircraft that virtually never require refueling – ideas of which were largely abandoned more than 50 years ago because of the dangers and complexities involved with nuclear fission reactors.

Yet the idea of nuclear fusion, in which atoms combine into more stable forms and release excess energy in the process, is not new. Ever since the 1920s, when it was postulated that fusion powers the stars, scientists have struggled to develop a truly practical means of harnessing this form of energy.

Other research institutions, laboratories and companies around the world are also pursuing ideas for fusion power, but none have gone beyond the experimental stage. With just a "Holy Grail" breakthrough seemingly within its grasp, and to help achieve a potentially paradigm shifting development in global energy, Lockheed has made public its project with the aim of attracting partners, resources and additional researchers."

Not having focused on the development of nuclear fusion before instead of the focus on dangerous nuclear power instead is a tragic mistake.

Nuclear power is dangerous and out of control

Advocates label nuclear power as a clean and safe form of energy. And again we see the danger of the work of people with a disconnected mind.

In real life it turns out the problems with the production of nuclear power are dangerous and out of control.

There are more and more signs that such a great amount of nuclear waste is present in the atmosphere that it weakens our immune systems, and it could lead to earlier development of Alzheimer's in people, among other things.

The public does not know about the countless risks of nuclear power and incidents that happened in nuclear power plants across the globe.

In the book *Les jeux de l'atome et du hasard* by Jean-Pierre Pharabod and Jean-Paul Schapira you can find an overview of officially acknowledged nuclear power accidents since 1988.

There is convincing evidence for the fact that no one has thoroughly mastered this technology: not a single state knows how to deal with serious accidents, the waste disposal issue seems unsolvable, dismantling it would cause countless problems, let alone issues like rivers heating up, or supervision of plutonium 239 (that stays radio-active for 100.000 years!). And lastly, even though nuclear reactors don't produce greenhouse gases, emissions from the whole nuclear cycle (exploitation, refining, fuel burn-off, and construction, operation, dismantling of plants, and waste disposal and storage) are not in the least negligible aspects. On average, the power plant that uses uranium 235 produces three times less emission as a regular gas-fuelled power station. The odds may be in favor of nuclear power now, however this will change in the future.

During extraction and processing of uranium the level of carbon dioxide emissions depend on the uranium content in the ore. Because uranium reserves shrink an increasing amount of energy will be wasted on extraction and exploitation, thus the level of carbon dioxide will rise accordingly. Lastly, remember the heat wave of 2003. The reactors could not be cooled down due to the high temperature of the rivers. This led to a shut-down of countless plants, leaving the population without electricity and as a consequence without air conditioning. The meteorological predictions mentioned in preceding chapters that point to a growing number of heat waves in the coming decennia, could be food for thought.

What's even worse, a few engineers have discovered that these same rivers might freeze, which could cause similar problems in cold seasons, when there is a sharp rise in the demand for heating…" (From: *Demain la Terre,* by Yannick Monget.)

You would expect that after the latest horrible nuclear disaster in Fukushima – the problems of which are anything but solved and the consequences anything but accounted for – the world would have woken up already, but alas…

Radioactive material still leaks from the Fukushima nuclear plant into the sea, spreading across the globe.

The current high amount of radioactive substances that has ended up in the ocean results in the fact that even the levels at the Miami coastline are too high. On top of that, radioactive substances have also been discovered higher up in the air. Certain symptoms (including certain skin conditions) suffered by pilots on intercontinental flights are being associated with these substances.

The fact that Japan refused access to international experts to solve the problems after this tragic nuclear disaster reveals an incredible lack of true insight. International intervention is absolutely crucial! It's a matter of life and death! Unfortunately, the tragic accident in Japan has not been the eye-opener to cut down on nuclear energy. In fact, one of the Fukushima power stations has been reactivated.

The only nation so far being courageous enough to cut down on nuclear power has been Germany!

Meanwhile, problems keep on emerging! In Belgium, 3 out of 7 nuclear power stations have been closed down after hairline cracks were discovered in the walls.

September 2015:

Thiange 1 is holding quiet again after 3 days in use.

Thiange 2 is already quiet for 2 years.

Thiange 3 is in August this year holding quiet again after being two weeks in use.

In June 2017, about 50.000 people made a human chain of 90 kilometers to protest against the dangerous unsafeness of the nuclear power stations in Thiange.

The chain started in Aachen (Germany) passed along Maastricht (Holland) and ended in Belgium. This action shows how worried and angry these people are!

Become a warrior for climate change

We have to convert our powerlessness into focused actions to solve the climate crisis together. Stand up, be heard and change your lifestyle. Become a climate change warrior like Wen

Stephenson. He worried to the extent that he quit his job in journalism and wrote an open letter to his colleagues, because the mainstream media keeps almost completely silent while climate scientists become increasingly alarmed. He literally asked his colleagues:

"Whose side are you on? Are you on the side of your fellow men? Then it's time to put the cards on the table and tell the public about the seriousness, extent and urgency of the crisis we are facing and what is to be done about it.

As a human being with a conscience-whose side do you choose? If you can't be honest, then exactly what is your role in this sector? Why are you a journalist? How can you look yourself in the eyes? And how can you look your children, grandchildren - or any other child - straight in the eyes?" Source: www.thephoenix.com / **Share Nederland**, December 2012

Become a warrior for climate change like the former president of the Republic of Ireland, Mary Robinson.

During the recent annual conference of the International Bar Association, she emphasized that the public has so strongly urged its political leaders to take direct action against the changes in our climate. Climate change is about to become one of the major injustices we will leave our children, grandchildren and great-grandchildren!

Source: Irish Independent / **Share Nederland**, November 2012.

Become a climate change warrior, just like the brave Naomi Klein, drawing a lot of attention with her interesting book called 'No time, this changes everything'. Her previous books (including 'No Logo', providing a critical analysis of globalization, and 'The Shockdoctrin', cleverly unmasking disaster capitalism and the destruction it has caused throughout the world for the past decades) show her excellent qualities as an investigative journalist.

In 'No Time' she explains why our current lifestyle cannot be reconciled with a livable earth for our future generations. It becomes more and more evident that 80% of the global warming is caused by human actions.

Preliminary information reveals that the level of greenhouse gas emissions was 61% higher in 2013 than in 1990. Current estimates show that the average temperature on earth has already increased with 0.8 degrees Celsius. This leads to many shocking results, including the melting of Greenland's ice cap and ocean acidification.

The consequences are developing way faster than expected.

According to a World Bank report from 2012, this means that the rising temperatures will result in many unexpected events with unpredictable consequences. Once we make the temperature rise up to a certain point, the process is irreversible. In other words, a temporary intervention will not do the job; we will have to do everything in our power to avoid the process to take an irreversible turn.

On the 25th of July 2015, I heard on the news that 17 leading climate scientists, under the leadership of James Hansen, wrote a 120-page report, revealing the fact that Greenland's ice caps are melting in a much faster pace than expected, that the sea level will rise quicker than predicted and that there will be a lot more floods and storms in the coastal areas. The days of symptoms treatment (increase the height of the dikes or the coastal areas) are over. The situation has become so serious that; we are forced to take all measures to achieve a responsible and sustainable lifestyle, as mentioned in this chapter, as soon as possible.

By the current increase in the sea level, many island States in the California Sea, the South Pacific and the Indian Ocean are threatened including the famous Tonga Islands and Clipperton Island.

This lot includes the 311.000 inhabitants of the Maldives. The Administrator members of the Tuvalu Islands (halfway between Hawaii and Australia) have already admitted that they have lost the fight against the rising waters and are passed to the evacuation of 11.000 people. Environmental refugees of these islands are already taken care of by New Zealand since 2002, after Australia had refused them.

Bangladesh is also threatened, there are already 4.7 million inhabitants who fled. This is an example of climate injustice.

According to Naomi Klein the assumption is that a 2 degrees Celsius rise is the turning point; a temperature that cannot be exceeded, based on leaving today's economic, competitive and exploiting model, and the increasingly dangerous methods of fuel generation (of which 'fracking', the hydraulic fracturing of underground rock layers is the most worrying) the way they are. She states: "what the climate needs is for humanity to reduce the raw material consumption." She discusses all kinds of steps to be taken, including the gradual cessation of subsidies for fossil fuels. According to a conservative estimate by Oil Change International and the Natural Resources Defense, this will save the government 775 billion dollar a year. 50 Dollar taxes for each ton of CO_2 emission in the developed countries, on the other hand, will bring in 450 billion a year (revealed by a report by, amongst others, the World Bank and the International Monetary Fund).

The 'Heartland Institute, a think-tank from Chicago committed to the stimulation of free market solutions, organizes annual conferences where they claim that greed and unlimited profit seeking have a bigger chance on increasing the world's emancipation than the world has ever had. Doubting the free market ideology is considered heresy and their actual scope is unexpected; some of the most leading environmental organizations, including the World Wildlife Fund, are connected to, and get subsidy from, companies like Shell, BP, Mobil and even WalMart and Monsanto. It's in their interest to maintain the current status quo so they organize effective campaigns full of incorrect information on global warming.

Despite the facts are not being hopeful, Klein is positive about the following: the failure of top-down, slick environment organizations and VN top-conferences led to more and more worried youngsters who joined BLOCKADIA.

This is a broad movement fighting against generating fossil fuels. It has become an incredibly vast network. (Source: **Share Nederland** Jan. Feb. 2015).

"I think it's unbelievable how the Heartland Institute encourages greed and unlimited profit seeking, and claims it will stimulate emancipation, while the opposite is true. These mechanisms will only make the rich richer and the poor poorer! The increasing inequality will make the level of anxiety in society rise. And today's production processes are increasingly polluting our planet and damage our health. In addition, the global warming caused a climate that is completely out of control, which has disastrous consequences."

America and China are the largest polluters and I am annoyed to the way the Republicans and Tea-party are tackling the problem of global warming and use their power and money to convince the public opinions.

They pay rogue scientists to disseminate false information. But their game is over, on the basis of the documentary: "Merchants in doubt" Robert Kenner and Naomi Oresker blame the fossil fuel lobby for deception and they advocate damage claims.

Unfortunately the American people made a choice for the wrong president because Donald Trump does not believe in climate change and he signed a decree to ignore the climate-agreement made in Paris to reduce the global warming.

The democrats are fighting back and lodged a juridical complaint against him. I hope they will win!

In the Netherlands, a worried group of civilians, united in the climate organization 'Urgenda', have ambitious plans: Under the inspiring leadership of Marjan Minnesma, they want Holland to be fossil-free in 2030. They decided to accuse the government for not taking appropriate action to fight the climate crisis, it sounds like a great initiative:

Urgenda won the law suit, and the court house confirmed the Dutch Government's climate policy has failed.

The court obliged them to take decisive measures, but the Dutch government considered appealed against this decision.

That makes me so desperate. I would like to shout it out from the rooftops: **WAKE UP AND SAVE OUR PLANET!!**

We urgently need an International Criminal Court, a tribunal with far-reaching powers so that crimes against the environment can be heavily penalized. This does not concern only direct pollution, for example in the form of illegal

discharges of toxic waste, but also to take appropriate measures to further negligence of global warming.

In addition to a universal declaration of human rights, we also have a need for the rights of the earth.

The former president of the Common Council of the United Nations, Miguel d'Escoto, decided to formulate a Universal Declaration on the Common Good of the Earth and Humanity.

He consulted a wide range of statesmen and other powerful people and came up with the following basic assumptions:

'Mother Earth is composed of all the ecosystems in which she has generated a magnificent multiplicity of forms of life, all of them interdependent and complementary, making up the great community of life. As the earth generated life herself, she must be treated with dignity and has to be protected and cared for'.

'The earth is our joint inheritance and her products must be divided equally. We don't own the earth, we are her guests!!'

Professor Leonardo Boff (Theology and Ethics), co-designer of the Earth Charter, points out that our collective future is at stake and that the environmental crisis can lead to a disconcerting humanitarian and ecological catastrophe, one that needs an immediate intervention on a global scale. Therefore, we must create a general normative framework which prescribes values and which is exemplary.

Furthermore, it should provide us with an ethical and political foundation for a global community. (Source: Share, the Netherlands April / June 2010)

What on earth does humanity need to finally wake up? When do we finally realize that the only way to stop the global warming is to start living a natural, green, sustainable way of life!!

When will the heads of governments finally realise that drastic measures need to be taken in order to turn the tide!!

Furthermore, a sustainable policy will benefit the economy by creating new jobs. Doing nothing will cost an incredible amount of money.

This is a responsibility for both the left as well as the right wing political parties; they have to join forces in their mission to stop the global warming! First measure should be extra taxes on polluting products. Until humanity realizes the dangers of the climate crisis, this is a suitable measure. As soon as humanity realizes that the polluter pays the price, awareness will be encouraged.

Far-reaching measures must therefore be taken to fight the environmental crisis on a global scale.

Become a warrior for climate change and become aware of your lifestyle and its impact on the climate of our earth. Do you choose to contribute to further destruction, or to the rebuilding of an ecological infrastructure? Use social media to call on others to become aware of their actions.

Finally and this is very important! Put as much pressure on politics to take adequate measures to solve the climate crisis.

SUSTAINABLE SOLUTIONS

It's all about creating truly sustainable, efficient solutions for our global problems instead of continuing the present hare-brained, short-term policies that supports the old polluting sick-making economy.

We only have a few decennia to repair the tremendous environmental damage we have inflicted, or else our own lives are at stake. We are facing an enormous challenge to make a radical change and choose sustainable production methods by opting for renewable 'green' energy. It's all possible! Germany is the ultimate proof! This country has taken some courageous decisions.

Looking at Germany we can see that these goals can be achieved. They made some right choices by cutting back on nuclear power, and raising consumption of solar power as well as wind power. In the whole of Europe their economy is one of the most successful ones. A high percentage of the labour force is employed in middle-sized businesses, often family owned, and in many cases those businesses still take great pride in their workmanship. Many people their vote in favour of green politics and there have been massive protests against nuclear power. Germany is Europe's largest producer of herbal medicine like homeopathy phytotherapy, and the ingenious bio resonance therapy. The Germans are an inspiring example for the world!

Ms. Angela Merkel, who steers Germany through this great 'Energiewende' with a steady hand, is a paragon of a very able and wise politician. She has a connected mind; her heart and mind are connected.

Luckily we see more and more of these connected minds among men of the younger generation, which gives hope for the future.

But there is a country in Europe that Germany still exceeds, and that is Denmark. Under the inspiring guide of Martin Lindegaard (ex-Minister of energy) Denmark has gone from 42% to 55% renewable energy in a short time. Denmark is a league leader in Europe; they are the largest exporters of green energy and have the most innovation projects. The Danish windmill industry is very successful and they are also no. 1 in the solar energy sector, so you see that switching to sustainable energy is not only good for the climate but also for the economy and employment.

Cradle tot cradle concept

The collaboration between the German chemist Michael Braungart and the American architect William McDonough is an excellent example. They met at a reception in New York, and were annoyed by the noise and smell of the cars in the streets in the city.

They philosophized about a world with exclusively clean, silent cars, and wrote the ground-breaking book *Cradle to Cradle* together.

This duo encourages us to design our products in such an intelligent way that product materials can be returned to organic and technical processes in order to use them again. This will result in eco-effective and clean production processes.

In short, this means that all raw materials can be reused and won't go to waste. That should be the starting point for all new products.

Synthetic products should be completely recyclable. After use they should be ground into bits, so the remaining granulate can serve as a component of new products. Their motto is: *Waste is food*. This is an entirely different point of departure compared to the present practice. Too many materials are unsuitable for recycling, and end up in the refuse incinerator or dump. This is called the cradle-to-grave principle, the reason for the unnecessary loss of too many possible starting components.

All sustainability is local

Only if we realize that all sustainability (and this applies to politics as well) is based in the local field, we can begin to fit in human systems and industries. Then we link them to local raw materials, local energy flows, and local customs, needs and tastes from a molecular to a regional level. We observe if and how the chemicals that we use impact the water and land quality (how could they be utilized as nourishing instead of polluting agents?) out of which the product is produced, and how our processes interact with the start and end of the supply chain. We will also investigate how we can create useful jobs, improve the economical and physical conditions in the area, and achieve ecological and technical prosperity in the future. If we import some material from a faraway place we also consider what happened on the other side of the world, and respect it as a local event elsewhere. This duo practice what they preach, and for instance have changed the polluted terrain of the Ford factories in Detroit into an ecological park with its own water purification facility. The factory halls have been fixed thoroughly, and appropriately adjusted to the people who work there. (From: *Duurzaam ontwikkelen... een wereldkans*, by Anne-Marie Rakhorst.)

I recommend this amazing book to everyone since in *Cradle to cradle*, Braungart and McDonough offer us an overall concept.

I put my faith in designers and inventors who come up with sustainable solutions for our problems and develop new forms of sustainable energy, and I give you some inspiring examples of innovators:

REVOLUTIONARY SUSTAINABLE INVENTIONS

Blue energy: energy derived from salt and fresh water

A new form of sustainable energy has been developed. It relies on the difference in salt content in fresh and salt water. It is called Blue Energy and for The Netherlands, a country abounding in water, it may turn out to be the perfect energy source.

Generating energy where salt and fresh water come together; The Netherlands contains many of these places. An example is the famous enclosure dam called the 'Afsluitdijk', and other places where fresh inland water level is kept lower than the salt seawater by using sluices. This system could generate almost enough energy for the entire country. Kees van den Ende, one of the KEMA scientists that are involved in the Blue Energy project says: 'If we are able to generate the energy in a financially acceptable way, this could be hugely beneficial to The Netherlands. Fifteen years ago, they already worked out that the amount of energy generated this way will be enough to serve the entire Dutch energy supply'.

Blue Energy relies on the difference in salt content between seawater and fresh water. Usually, these waters blend where they come together but if a plastic membrane (a kind of filter) is placed in between, energy can be generated. Van den Ende: 'The used technique is called reverse electro dialysis. Salt consists of positively and negatively charged ions. If salt and fresh water are blended using special membranes, the plus ions are sent to one direction and the minus ions the other. Then, the water on one side of the membrane is positively charged, the water on the other side is negatively charged, which makes it possible to use the principles of a battery: by placing two bars and attaching a wire in between, current can flow.'

Van den Ende: *'Our method completely depends on the price of the membrane. Only for the 'Afsluitdijk' power station we need five to ten square kilometres of membranes. Fifteen years ago, membranes were only available in the medical industry. These membranes were way too expensive. In the past five years, the prices have dropped but we, together with our partners, are still aiming for more economic membranes.'*

Daan Roosegaarde

There is one Dutch innovator who to me is incredibly interesting and inspiring. He is called Daan Roosegaarde and he develops all kinds of sustainable solutions using magical special effects with light.

This successful designer developed glow-in-the-dark paint that can be used for road markings. He received worldwide press coverage by winning the Danish Index Award in 2013 with his 'Smart Highway Project'. Besides this, he developed something similar to a hoover, creating a weak magnetic field that pulls the smog downwards, giving people in the big cities that are suffering from high levels of smog the chance to temporarily 'catch their breath'. On top of that, this C2C man uses this dirty smog waste to make rings. Recently, he designed a magical light spectacle in Amsterdam. To passersby it seemed as if the area was flooded by water. He aimed to warn people for the danger of the rising sea level. Daan is buzzing with energy and has many other plans.

Currently, he is busy developing a smart electronic car that is able to charge itself on the road.

Pieter Hoff

In 2010, another fellow countryman won an eco-price with his amazing important invention, the 'waterboxx'. His name is Pieter Hoff and he invented a system that allows us to plant trees in dry areas using a cardboard pot with a hole in the bottom. The pot contains a wick that is planted into the soil via the hole in the bottom, which allows gradually small amounts of 50 mm of water to reach the roots. This system provides the young tree with the best chances of growth.

Boyan Slat

Finally, the Dutch Boyan Slat deserves to be mentioned and honoured for his invention of a device with giant floating arms, being a few kilometres long, deleting the plastic out of the ocean. Nowadays he has drawn international attention and an organisation called 'The Ocean Cleanup' was founded around him. Currently, he is doing research using 30 sailing ships in The Great Pacific Garbage Patch; an area located between Hawaii and California containing huge amounts of plastic waste.

Lex Hoeksloot and Tessie Hartjes

But there is more exciting news: Lex and Tessie are producing an ingenious electric car, the Lightyear one, that charges itself with sunlight. This car is provided with a battery and thus continuously supplied with solar power.

More info: www.lightyear.one

Sean Lee Davis

Revolutionary inventions, however, are not just a contribution of the Dutch. Amazing initiatives are launched throughout the whole world. I truly enjoyed watching a documentary called 'Fill my tank' about Sean Lee Davis driving from Malaysia to Cambodia using used cooking oil which he collected at restaurants along the way. An ingenious converter (designed by Andrew Kan) in his car converted the cooking oil into bio fuel within 1.5 to 2 hours. Along the way, he visited all kinds of eco-projects such as an ingenious factory run by Jack Ling in Malaysia, converting waste oil into bio fuel, and an eco-resort in Cambodia run by a Frenchman called Matthieu, who built an amazing swimming pool based on a German concept. The water was purified by water plants lined up along the pool. It looked like a little paradise. After his long and adventurous trip came to an end, he donated his converter to a children's home called 'Sunrise Children Village'.

Elon Reeve Musk

The well known, very creative inventor Elon Reeve Musk is among other things the founder of Space X and he became famous with the design of the best sold ingenious electric car, the Tesla.

At the moment he works out a so called 'Hyperloop', a high speed-tubular-transport-system. In the tube there will be 'capsules' with the size of a car and they move with a speed of 1200 kilometres in one hour.

Mr. Keneyeres

And let's not forget about other ecological projects that were realised in the past, such as the magnificent botanic garden in Budapest founded by Mr. Keneyeres where the waste of half a million people is converted into biogas and where the water of these people is purified.

All these magnificent and educational projects truly make me happy! Now I can only hope that, within a short period of time, designers come up with a formula to cool the ice in Greenland for as long as humanity doesn't wake up and keeps on warming our globe.

PIERRE RHABI'S SEVEN STEP PROGRAM (from: *Demain la terre*, Yannick Monget)

Luckily there are genuinely efficient solutions available in the fields of energy, with wind and solar power, and also nutrition such as the reintroduction of agro ecology in France, thanks to Pierre Rhabi. It involves, at times, incredibly simple solutions in which the environment is taken into consideration. Direct application of this seven-step programme in our societies as soon as possible would be a wise course of action.

Label all products (food, domestic appliances, etc., indicating the effects on health and environment) so consumers will be able to make a conscious choice.

EDUCATE THE MASSES IN ORDER TO

- Initially limit their energy consumption

- Make knowledgeable choices, buy healthy, non-polluted
  products that respect the ecosystems

IN AGRICULTURE

- Strictly prohibit GMO crops
- Impose sensible use of fresh water supplies
- Abolish pesticides and use natural weed killers instead
- Produce and consume organic products (this way we
  contribute to lowering prices)
- Develop sustainable agriculture with the help of subsidies
  Stimulate crop rotation for more efficient use of farmland
  Plant trees in fields and corn-growing, to improve the yield.

IN TRANSPORT

- Build more road-rail transport facilities Promote public
  transport
- Encourage carpooling
- Promote use of alternative, non-polluting means of
  transport (bikes, etc.).
- Develop new non-polluting engines that run on clean
  energy fuels (bio fuel, electric motor, etc.), and build
  matching infrastructures for cities and households (for
  recharging electric cars, among other things)

IN CONSTRUCTION

- Pay attention to clever isolation (limit energy loss in
  heating systems and noise pollution, etc.)
- Plant vast green spaces in cities, plant gardens on

rooftops that fight urban pollution (the infamous smog), and ensure a drop in local temperatures. Improve the use of streetlights in towns at night

IN NATURAL ENVIRONMENTS

- Initiate massive reforestation and create new opportunities for carbon storage, and carbon dioxide reduction. Create new flood - preventing wet lands. Build ecological parks, protect and reintroduce endangered species, downsize hunting and fishing areas.

IN POLITICS

- Extend the authority of the Ministry of Infrastructure and Environment, and make it the most important one together with the Ministry of Education, Culture, and Science.
- Expose the differences between north and south, especially in Africa and India, and offer support and relief
- Help these developed countries to opt for solutions based on sustainable energy, and cancel their debts right now. Then they have more means available for additional ecological measures.
- "The Tripartite Pact (scientists, industrialists, governments) is crucial in order for the earth to recover, or else nothing will change." (Hubert Reeves, *Mal de Terre,* 1999)

IN TECHNOLOGY

- Drain thermal power station's carbonic acid gas directly into the ocean.
- Use solar power (solar cells, solar updraft towers, parabolic reflectors), and wind power.
- Extend the application of hydrogen, that together with oxygen turns into water. Expand the uses of biomass. (This is not always sustainable energy. M.F.)
- Piecemeal replacement of coal-power stations for new types of installations (for example wind turbines)

In the meantime we should fight waste on all fronts

We are wasting incredible amounts of food since we're importing and exporting it to the end of the world and back. The demands regarding the appearance of the food are getting more and more absurd. The tomato and the potato, for instance, need to have a perfect round or oval shape. An imperfect shape is not accepted. We also throw out a large, unnecessary amount of food ourselves. The supermarkets sell everything in family sizes and forget about people that live alone. In addition, for all this transport, a huge amount of fuel is needed. Every country should grow its own food as much as possible. Only the extra necessary products should be imported. It has been proven that locally grown food contains the most energy and power to keep people healthy. We also waste an incredible amount of raw materials because tricky and smart advertising campaigns encourage us to follow the latest trends in order to outstrip others. We all want the trendiest car, design, furniture, fashion, television, mobile phone or PC. Whether all this design is functional doesn't seem to be important anymore. I, personally, am extremely annoyed by the irregular bottoms of design mineral water bottles that keep on falling over. And by design cars with trendy higher placed side-windows which make reverse parking so much harder. I try to ignore trends wherever I can. I buy twenties and thirties style furniture in second hand shops and I used to buy second hand clothes. I'm only fashion forward when I really like something. It doesn't interest me at all whether other people like it or not.

All our consumables are produced for a short life. This used to be different. In the old days, sustainable, solid products were made for long-term usage. The very first light bulb, for instance, would work for 2500 hours.

Finally Anne-Marie Rakhorst gives many valuable tips. Below you find a brief selection.

FOR THE CONSUMERS

- Purchase a HRE boiler (high efficiency boiler) when your boiler needs to be replaced;
- Join an energy company that supplies both green electricity and green gas; Have your regular light bulbs replaced by low energy light bulbs, or even better, by LED lighting;
- Use your bike (or public transportation – M.F.) instead of your car; Buy a hybrid car;
- Join a 'sustainable' and carbon neutral bank;
- With every product you buy, ask the retailer or manufacturer whether it was produced in a sustainable and fair way, also to make them more aware;
- Make sure your home is well isolated and has double glazing;
- Make sure, when replacing old devices, to purchase energy-saving new ones, provided with an A-label;
- Install a water-saving showerhead;
- Have a diesel particulate filter fitted to your diesel vehicle;

- Check the options to jointly switch to solar or wind energy installations, or thermal storage;
- Grow your own crops and herbs in your garden or on your balcony;

FOR BUSINESS

- Discuss the advantages of a social committed life for people, their environment and the economy in your private and professional network → People, Planet, Profit. Don't think your opinion is not important. The higher the level of social commitment, the bigger the chance of a sustainable change;
- Keep on providing the government and business life with critical feedback and calling for action regarding their energy policy;
- Set up a sustainability platform with thinkers and doers (and innovative designers – M.F.) that helps the government establish an action plan;
- Encourage sustainable entrepreneurship and provide starting entrepreneurs with tax benefits (this also results in more work – M.F.);
- Make a profit with sustainable and carbon neutral entrepreneurship;
- As a government, you need to give the right example; accommodate politicians and civil servants in sustainable buildings and have them drive hybrid cars;
- Use video-conferencing in international business communication. The installation of a webcam on PCs, all parties involved are able to communicate 'face to face', which will reduce the needed amount of kerosene and petrol;

- Only use FSC-certified paper and printers;
- Have your corporate caterer only serve local products instead of all kinds of exotic vegetables and fruit.

Sustainable production, consuming less, and a more equal distribution of wealth are vital to provide the peace and happiness that everyone is longing for. I'm asking everyone to help carry out this vast process of transformation on our planet Mother Earth.

THE REVOLUTION OF THE SUSTAINABLE-CIRCULAR ECONOMY

With the motto 'back to basic: a simple life is a happy life' an alternative global economy emerges, also known as a share economy. It is based on selling fair trade and local products without intermediate trade or commission brokers.

Remember the brilliant 'cradle-to-cradle' concept of Braungart & Mc. Donough: Only if we realize that all sustainability is local, we can start to fit it in human systems and industries and: All raw materials can be reused. That should be starting point for all new products.

Luckily, more and more people are starting to wake up. Collaborations striving for more control over our basic needs are emerging everywhere. This mostly concerns the production of fair trade and organic food and renewable energy. More and more people are setting up a collective to jointly buy solar panels.

Naomi Klein draws attention to a German initiative revolving around hundreds of councils taking back control over their power supply. In Wiemersdorf, a town with a population of 26.000

people, they managed to produce clean energy without subsidy. But also all kinds of swapping initiatives are being developed. These services involve using each other's houses and cars or services including babysitting, refurbishing and cooking services. Sometimes small financial compensations are requested.

People grow tired of intensive farming and factory farming products and fake food fraud like the horsemeat scandal. They grow more and more aware of the fact that the regular foods on the market are not very good for them due to their high levels of sugar, salt, trans fats, and artificial additives they contain.

The demand for organic food keeps growing, and people have started cultivating their own allotments and kitchen gardens. Ex-first Lady Michelle Obama gave a good an example here.

Besides this, the number of initiatives providing small-scale day-care services for children and elderly homecare management is growing.

In Germany, an amazing project has been realised. The project is based on a so-called 'Mehr-Genarationen-Haus'. This house is a meeting point for three generations children, grown-ups and elderly people to meet up and do things together. The house also provides room for unemployed people and troubled youngsters. Currently, 450 of these houses have been realised. To some of them (depending on their size) a kitchen, small restaurant or even shops are added.

The project turned out to be such a great success, the German government decided to donate 16 million Euros. This means 30.000 Euros for each house! This is a brilliant way to fight the social isolation amongst elderly people.

Recent Dutch research shows that half of the elderly in Rotterdam feels lonely. In fact, 25% of the elderly people haven't got anyone to turn to at all. Last year, the body of a woman was found. It turned out that her dead body had been lying there for ten years.

This is the result of the increasing individualisation, commercialised healthcare and the busy, overburdened lives of their children and grandchildren. Care homes for the elderly as we used to know them are being shut down fast. Only the elderly people that are ill or in need of help are admitted to nursing homes. Also, major cutbacks in district nursing and social care are being realised.

Recently, I saw geriatricians raise alarm in Holland. Elderly people in need are often forced to stay in the hospitals for weeks, sometimes even months, longer than necessary, for there is no room for them in the nursing homes. They are pushed to go back home even though they are scared and in need of help. In my opinion, these are disgraceful practices taking place in one of the wealthiest countries in the world.

We are talking about vulnerable people who lived through World War II and helped re-building the country.

That's why I feel so passionate about the German 'Mehr-Generationen-Haus' project. Many more similar projects should be established to realise easy accessible meeting points.

Whenever I am in Holland, I visit an incredible place myself. It is called 'De Buurtboerderij' (which means The Community Farm) and is located just outside Amsterdam. The project consists of an old, renovated farm with a restaurant that allows people to have a 3-course meal for €5.

In the farm, all kinds of cultural events, such as music performances, are organised. There is a recycle shop where everything is free of charge (I found several very interesting books there). The farm is surrounded by magnificent gardens (including a herb and vegetable garden) and there is a sheep pen. There are terraces all over the place where people are able to eat lovely outside and build a campfire. It's an idyllic place, a sanctuary for friendship and creativity!

DETERIORATION OF THE POSITION OF EMPLOYEES

In our current 'post-capitalistic' era the position of workers is getting worse. Many people are fired because more and more companies decide to move their business to low-wage countries.

In the south of Europe, nearly half of the young labour force is already unemployed.

If such a large amount of young people are no longer able to earn a living and have lost all hope for a better future, something in the social structure is seriously wrong. This leads to aimlessness and boredom, which on their turn lead to alcoholism, drug abuse and senseless violence.

Europe hardly does anything to solve this problem and their policy is very hard to understand; they are forcing elderly people to work until they are 67 years of age. Older people have completed their duty and deserve their rest in order to enjoy their old age (as far as their circumstances allow them to).

I've always been against the abrupt start of retirement; a system where people are still working full time one day, whereas the next day they are full time retired pensioners. Why not give people who have reached the age of 65 freedom of choice in deciding whether they still have the energy and spirit to work. After reaching the age of 60, many people feel their energy level dropping while the level of physical diseases rises. Therefore, I advocate a gradual decrease of working hours for older people using a part-time working schedule.

Recent research has shown that both employers and older workers are dissatisfied with this policy which has mainly been affected to reduce pension benefits, but in practice it does not.

Besides this, politics should be focusing on an effective solution for youth unemployment. More jobs should be created for young people. Education should be increasingly adjusted to their needs and future jobs. In addition, young people receiving unemployment benefits should be doing voluntary work in return.

The contract periods in countries where young people can still get a job, including the Netherlands, are getting increasingly shorter. The extremely high work pressure results in a longterm burn-out for over 10% of young employees.

Specially for the older employees (and you are already old when you are 55+) it is difficult to find another job. They are forced to apply for another job but most of all they don't even reserve an answer on their applications. At the end they are without courage and desperate. They fall back financially to unemployment benefit and go backward the longer they stay unemployed. At the end they are dependent of the poor-relief and food-supply and in the worst case they become homeless. This a really a big abuse that has to be tackled: It is unacceptable that employees who worked hard and devoted for their companies are thrown away without a good supply-arrangement.

In the past an employee who performed well in his new job could get a steady contract after a period of probation. This contract gave the security to ground a family, to buy a house, etc. Nowadays there is little security because there is a lot of flex-work and this creates fear for the future.

In Holland for instance one out of three jobs are based on temporarily flex-contracts. The workers receive less wage, they have less right to internal training and they have more fear to give their opinion. Many companies (specially the small ones) fire their flex-workers within two years, because afterwards they have to give them a steady contract.

In Holland there are also a lot of so called ZZP-workers [self-employed / freelancer] that means people who run their business alone without personnel. They also have a bad position without insurance and perspective to build up a retired pay.

In Denmark they take better care of their flex-workers. If they lose their flex-job they receive a good payment and they can count on an intensive accompaniment to be trained and even prepared to switch over to another type of work.

This method is very successful and a model for the rest of Europe.

But also the employees who are still active in the field can hardly correspond to all the changes and have to refresh their knowledge. There are even institutes like the General Assembly in London that offers for a lot of money training-courses for the highly educated to remain up-to-date employees.

The future-prospect is not very hopeful. Because of digitalization automation and robotics more and more jobs will be lost and we must prepare our self that there will not be enough paid work for all of us. We have to find alternative ways to create over our work and there is more pleading to give everyone a minimal basic-income.

On the other hand there are also positive examples of flexible work by which the employees experience more freedom:

SUSTAINABLE ENTREPRENEURSHIP & FLEXIBLE WORK STRUCTURE

Currently we find ourselves in an exciting time of transition. The old top-model consisting of a hierarchic business structure has had its day. The fact that employees are contributing to the success of the company while the rewards for the board of management are completely out of proportion is no longer accepted. Specially young people have a strong need to start their own business specially 'online'.

The administrative rigmarole to realize this should be simplified and banks should offer more credits to young starting entrepreneurs. Many young people now choose to take control of their own destiny by setting up crowd-funding actions.

Thanks to the spectacular invention of the 3d printer, decentralization will increase and the power of the big companies will decline. More and more companies will get rid of the old hierarchy and equally divide the financial results over the employees.

There are interesting experiments with flexible working hours where employees can decide whenever they come and go to perform a certain amount of work. If they achieve well, they can even get a longer holiday period. The results are very good, especially in Sweden where young fathers even a half year leave to help with the care of newborn babies. In Sweden they did an experiment with a working day of six hours and the productivity was high and the workers were very happy. There are also experiments where you can come and go whenever you want as long you fulfil your targets. This will relieve the peak hours in the traffic and save a lot of time being blocked on the highway.

Another documentary of 'Tegenlicht' showed a huge transition, taking place currently, ending the old and cold efficient business structure and building up a new structure where human beings take up a central role. A structure where human abilities and contribution are being respected and trusted.

Jan Rotmans, professor of Transition and Transition Management, states that we need fresh thinkers, dissenters and uniters in order to build up a new, sustainable and intelligent society.

He says that around 250.000 people are busy building this new order and his goal is to raise this amount to 2.5 million people within five years; at that point the tipping point is reached. (The Netherlands has about 17 million people).

An increasing amount of employees start their own cooperatives, creating their own working methods; people on the shop floor often have brilliant ideas. No management and overhead is needed; the profit goes directly to the employees.

We urgently need the creation of a circular-sustainable economy to fight against climate change.

There are more and more big companies and even multi-nationals who feel a need to make a transition from linear to circular economy and to save our climate.

Thank goodness we see everywhere in the world a growing awareness of sustainable living. This is very hopeful for the future!

Transition Towns (also known as the transition network or transition movements) have begun to spread worldwide.

Transition Towns is a grass root network of volunteers and communities whose main aim is to raise awareness of sustainable living and build local ecological resilience in the near future. The supporters of transition towns are driven by climate change and the depletion of oil and other fossil fuels. By now, there are more than a thousand local transition communities. Within two years local participants have succeeded in reducing their energy consumption by 20%. In addition the transition town initiatives are strengthening the community spirit. For more information see: http://www.transitiontowns.nl Source: **Share Nederland**, March 2013.

There is even an alternative-money system:

Barter is booming and battering systems are becoming increasingly popular as well as different types of mutual services. Even alternative or complementary currencies and monetary systems are appearing all over the world. In The Netherlands, for instance, they created the Makkie, an alternative currency in order to reward the inhabitants of the Amsterdam East area for their community work. Canada has the Kawartha Loon Exchange or KLE, an initiative by Transition Towns Peterborough. The KLE oversees an organized system of exchange between local producers, retailers and consumers, primarily for life-essential goods and services.

In Bristol city, in the south of England, with over 400,000 inhabitants they have got the Bristol pound. The passionate Mayor George Ferguson has tuned Bristol into 'the green capital of Europe', containing its own power station and all kinds of co-operatives in the area growing healthy food to supply the supermarkets in town. His slogan is: "You cannot produce a good city without breaking rules".

The big companies and specially the multinationals need to be more sustainable and abandon their extremely high profits to save our climate.

Anne-Marie Rakhorst investigated how green dreams could be financed and she proved that a circular-sustainable economy offers a good-profit-model. She tries to convince the financial sector in Holland. De Nederlandse Bank (The Dutch Bank) also advises to invest in sustainable projects!

In Holland a group of companies (under which the biggest five) did an urgent request to the Dutch government to create more facilities for sustainable entrepreneurship and climate legislation because Holland realized only 5% and this is a big shame for a prosperous country with a flourishing economy.

The Dutch Peter Bakker is the president of the world business council for sustainable developments. It does not help anymore to change a bit here and a bit there.

His slogan is: "We need a radical change!"

Jeffrey Sachs played a big role in the climate congress in Paris in 2015. He organized an international team of scientists and developed the "Deep decarbonisation project! His slogan is: "We have to get rid of coal, oil and gas; the DNA of our energy system has to change totally." He tried to convince the international government to support this project and take the right decisions in Paris. Jeffrey Sachs is advisor of Bank-i-moon.

IN THE FREE MARKET ECONOMY, FREEDOM IS AN ILLUSION!

The modern, hectic way of life in the industrial countries contradicts the basic principles for a healthy and happy life.

We THINK we are free but:

- Where is the freedom in being programmed to carry out
  routine work in factories and offices, 8 hours a day for
  about 45 years?
- Where is the freedom in being forced to work harder and
  harder because of the diminution of employees and the
  exploitation of the remaining workers to carry out the
  same work with less people, in order to make more
  profit?
- Where is the freedom in people buying houses in times of
  economic prosperity and banks offering them mortgages
  subject to favourable conditions? But what if you are
  being fired through no fault of your own which makes it
  impossible to pay the mortgage on one hand, and to sell
  the house on the other hand, because due to the credit
  crisis the sale is stagnating and the house price has
  dropped in value?
- And where is the freedom in being a European citizen
  and being forced to accept an entirely new money
  system, without a referendum?

Is that called living in a democracy? No, if such crucial decisions are taken without involving the people, we are living in a pseudo democracy.

Right now, for many people freedom is an illusion because we are all trapped in the so-called Free Market Economy. Freedom, for whom?

Certainly not for the millions of poor and hungry people on this planet. Neither for the managers that work like hell risking a heart attack!

FAILING POLITICIANS

Most political leaders are not capable to solve global problems. They are too much concerned with their own party's agenda and short-term planning, and rarely do not break their promises. Right-wing political leaders are too much in 'leading strings' of multi-nationals & banks-lobbies.

Let me get this straight: the government should ensure the quality of our basic facilities since this is one of the reasons we pay taxes. Right now European citizens are left too much at the mercy of the market forces.

Citizens must hold their governments accountable and take action if their governments fail in their primary task. As a way of political punishment, citizens should no longer vote for political parties that are supporting scrupulous lobby groups in order for these parties to lose their grip on society. In this respect, too many people are still unaware of this issue and lack the necessary understanding.

The difference between 'old-left' and 'new-right' in politics is fading and many people lost their trust and don't know anymore how to vote.

I can advice these doublers to vote for 'new-left-wing-parties who fight against climate-change-disasters and who are willing to realize a sustainable economy.

I have noticed that making policies is always about a choice between either this or that: either you choose to sympathize with liberals or left-wing parties, or you support conventional medicine or alternative medicine, etc.

In order to solve global problems the either/or viewpoints are too limited: we need and/and scenarios. The ideal social

structure consists of a new sustainable capitalism and socialism. The perfect health care system is achieved by combining both herbal medicine and conventional medicine.

Global problems can only be solved from an integral holistic vision that surpasses all restrictive dogmas.

Together we can break the power of the powerful lobbies and force them to change their policy. What we need – now more than ever – is a revolution of awareness!! Together we can bring pressure to bear on the politics to work for peace, health and happiness. Be inspired by all those courageous people all over the world who are already making an effort to live a natural, sustainable life. In this book you will find many examples of them.

Two remarkable warriors for a better world

There are 'two warriors' for a better world that stand out because they have revolutionary positions and pursuing radical changes.

1. Federico Zaragoza

The first one is Professor Federico Zaragoza, former director-general of UNESCO, who is now chairman of The Foundation for a Culture of Peace. He says that we can no longer be governed by the laws of the free market system, since they tend to be highly misleading.

The power of the globalizers has caused great damage and is responsible for the terrible crisis we are in today.

Now, more than ever, the developed countries exploit the lesser developed countries. Every day, four billion dollar is spent on armament, while over 60,000 people die of starvation each day (half of which are children). 80% of the world's wealth is distributed amongst only 20% of the total population, while the remaining 80% of the population can barely survive with only 20% of the remaining resources. Most of the time, they live in poor circumstances and attempt to reach the shores of the more developed countries, often fearing for their lives. Ethically, this is completely unacceptable and according to Zaragoza we are accomplices and therefore responsible for this 'unintended manslaughter'. Clearly, we find ourselves in a deep crisis. Which, however, also provides us with a major opportunity.

We have to take control of the future and join our forces in order for radical changes to be realised. We have to stand up and make clear that we no longer concur with an economy that is based on speculation, exploitation and warfare. It is about time a worldwide, large-scale mobilisation takes place.

The united nations should be reformed in order for all countries to be guided by the universal declaration of human rights. This way, both our culture and our economy can turn into a society that is based on solidarity, sustainable development, dialogue and peace.

Zaragoza keeps harping on the fact that remaining silent is more shameful than not speaking when you are silenced. (Source: Share, The Netherlands, July / August 2008).

Today, nine years later, the disparity is even greater. The Occupy Movement chanted that the ratio was 1%-99%.

A handful of billionaires are having the absolute power nowadays.

2. Pope Franciscus

The second one is the tireless new pope Franciscus. It is remarkable how the new Pope gets involved with politics, contrary to most of his predecessors.

He visited Lampedusa and in his lecture he spoke about everyone being indirectly responsible for the tragedy of the many drowned migrants. He mentioned the tyranny of the unrestrained capitalism and appealed to the world leaders to end the exploitation of the less developed world. In his eyes, the autonomy of the market and the speculation mechanism should be banned in order to distribute resources and wealth in an honest way. In addition, he appeals to the rich people on this planet to donate part of their capital to the less fortunate people.

I even heard that he once said that people that live in industrialized countries have a kind of 'existential schizophrenia' and 'spiritual Alzheimer'.

I don't know if this is true but in my eyes it is a brilliant metaphor that people who have a split between heart and mind are alienated from their True Self and are divided in sub-personalities with different 'needs and greeds'. He recently wrote an encyclical about the climate crisis and in September 2015 he held impressive speeches in the U.S. Congress and in the United Nations.

This great Pope always puts the emphasis on three topics:

1. **The destruction of nature and the ego-centric greed of the richer class.**
2. **The unequal distribution of money and goods.**
3. **The refugees who are desperately looking for a better life.**

I think this is extremely courageous and inspiring and I certainly hope this pope will be among us for a long time.

Be inspired by writers who converted Universal Wisdom into practical advice. Books like *Your Erroneous Zones* by Wayne Dyer and *Living in the Light* by Shakti Gawain really contributed to my personal development.

"Once we accept the higher power in the Universe reaching us through our intuition, we will realize that our personal problems and even problems on a global level occur since our intuition is not being respected. Personal and social problems are based on fear and the suppression of our intuition. We are not alone with our problems. We can trust our intuition like trusting an amazing and a wise friend, guiding us on our journey through life. A friend who helps and loves us. We can practice following our intuition knowing we are cared for and loved."

"I am always guided by my higher power" - Shakti Gawain

Today, you can take control of your own life and start your own process of self-knowledge and self-realization, and the development of self-love, and love for your fellow human beings and for our planet, 'Mother Earth'. That way, you are able to get in touch with your inner source of happiness again, that will guide you using wise, intuitive signs.

Basic rule for a sustainable way of life is to respect the universal intelligence that organizes the ingenious cycle of the ecological infra structure.

Follow your heart and use your head to realise the outcome of your heart-flow!

Our future depends on the level we are willing to wake up, make the right choices and carry out the right actions to

regain the control over our lifes. We have become way too apathetic and handed over too much of our power.

Mass apathy is dangerous for our democracy, which is turning into a pseudo-democracy already.

I INVITE EVERYONE TO WAKE UP, STAND UP AND HELP TO CREATE A REVOLUTION OF AWARENESS IN ORDER TO HEAL OURSELVES AND OUR SEVERELY DAMAGED PLANET.

In this book I give many examples of courageous people who work with heart and soul to create a better world. But there are more women, men, even children who are not named and they also have to be honoured.

AND TODAY YOU CAN DECIDE TO JOIN US!

People that participate in these kinds of projects experience a higher level of joy as it gives meaning to our lives and strengthens the community spirit.

The Universe seems to reward people that follow their heart.

CONTRIBUTING TO A BETTER WORLD IS THE MOST MEANINGFUL AND FULFILLING WORK IN THE WORLD!

Awareness, Insight, Targeted Action are the keys to sustainable happiness and radiant health.

Organic food, sustainable production, consuming less and a more equitable distribution of wealth; all vital elements to provide us with the radiant health sustainable happiness and peace that we are all longing for.

THE DOCUMENTARY HEALTH & HAPPINESS IN YOUR OWN HANDS

In the documentary Marianna combines the Universal wisdom about what makes us happy and worldwide research about what makes us healthy and slim, with the aim to help you free yourself step by step from your conditioned self and your subsequent stressful, unhealthy lifestyle. This will enable you to reconnect with your True Self, a centre of infinite creative consciousness.

Consciousness is the key that opens the door to liberation. You need to be liberated from all negative behavioural patterns that are harmful and limiting. And by using your creative power through positive thinking and visualization you can create a better future for yourself and your fellow humans.

1. Living from your own source of happiness

In this part Marianna explains that we are all born with the ability to be happy, our inner source of happiness. Unfortunately, we are cut off from this source, and we are told time and again that we can only be happy if we earn as much money as we possibly can. Marianna discusses how you can get in touch with our source of happiness again, and become self-aware and self-confident. We learn how to deal with negative behavioural patterns. And we learn how positive thinking and creative visualization can help us achieve our dreams.

2. Loving relationships

We do not learn how to properly love ourselves and others because we put great value on outward appearances. Advertising bombards us with absurd ideal images that cause us to get a negative self-image. Partners no longer have time for each other; parents are too busy to be proper guides for their children. In this part Marianna shows how you can tackle all of these social requirements and deal with yourself and your family members in a positive and loving way again, making your home a safe haven where you can be your True Self.

3. A healthy way of living

Our modern lives are characterized by an unhealthy and stressful lifestyle. More and more people resort to alcohol, tobacco, and drugs. We eat too much of the wrong foods (too much sugar and saturated fats), and use sleeping pills and antidepressants.

In this part Marianna maps out the damage. Before the Industrial Revolution Western diseases such as cancer, cardiovascular diseases, hypoglycaemia, and systemic candidiasis hardly ever occurred. Marianna shows by use of global research how you can stay healthy, slim and energetic throughout your life.

She explains the importance of balancing a diet of organic food and supplements to prevent geriatric conditions with an especially composed exercise programme. Marianna is an advocate of integral holistic medicine, and she takes you to a specialized health clinic.

4. Serious global problems and the solution

We are suffering more and more from the effects of the climate crisis, financial crisis, and expressions of religious delusion. Global power lies in the hands of banks and multinationals.

Humanity needs to make a choice. Either we all go down together because of our greed, personal gain of power and money, and abusing and exploiting the environment or we can create a better world based on solidarity and honest distribution of goods, while developing a sustainable production system.

According to Marianna we need a revolution of awareness, connecting people's minds and hearts, stop pointless wars, and take action and defy world powers by becoming as self-reliant as we can be, for example by making our buildings carbon neutral.

The DVDs are available on www.bol.com and on www.amazon.co.uk, de and it.

If you also worry about global problems, and you are dedicated to creating a better world, visit my web site www.blueprintforabetterworld.com.

Here you will find interesting articles. If you go to www. blueprintforabetterworld.com/video.htm

You will find a compilation of my documentary 'Health and Happiness in Your Own Hands'. If you share my views, please spread this information to as many people as possible through social media like Twitter, Facebook, etc.

Comments on the documentary by Marianna Farfalla: Blueprint for a better world, health and happiness in your own hands.

Rabbi Mordechal-Lazar, head of the monastery: *The holy church of Nativity' in Jerusalem: Message from Israel. 'Blueprint*

for a better world' is very inspiring and educational, and made with good intentions and knowledge. It's very good! Thank you.

Josephine Wall, artist from England: *Your ideas and hope for the world are admirable and I support you 100%.*

Reverend Dominic Egbe from Nigeria (Holy Church of God - Lagos): *You inspire me with 'Blueprint for a better world'. It is the best documentary ever made. Thank you very much and may God bless you.*

Karimi Azar on behalf of a group of women in Iran: *Thank you for the hope you bring into our lives with your documentary. Thanks for all the work and loving care you carried out into a world where many people are no longer involved. I hope people realize that the world will only get better when as many people as possible join forces.*

Gianfranco Serafini, director of a health clinic in Italy: *Marianna is a great speaker who really knows how to get to people. I am sure that with this documentary she will help many people and I am proud to have been part of this valuable project.*

Eddy Roos (artist) and **Maria v.d. Louw** (yoga teacher): *When we watched your documentary, we were very moved. What a great view on politics. You offer a real solution to world problems. If this was put into practice, the world would look better. Beautiful, very beautiful!*

Albert Bronk, journalist and life coach: *It's a great documentary, super. I enjoyed it. It was even better than I expected.*

Mariska Vroom, manager drugstore: *I admire Marianna and her commitment to nature. I thought it was a fantastic documentary and love that she raises this issue.*

Nahid Karimi, assistant chemist: *When I saw this impressive documentary, I felt that I should do something. It gave me a lot of positive energy. That's why I posted parts of it on my Facebook and I received many positive responses from Iran, such as my sisters.*

Karen Ooms, nurse: *I think your documentary is very inspirational and educational. You have given a lot of care and attention to it and everything comes straight from your heart. Many thanks and lots of respect for you.*

www.ingramcontent.com/pod-product-compliance
Lightning Source LLC
Chambersburg PA
CBHW051439250726
48655CB00001B/144